C000254815

DESMOND TUCKER was born in
his life, apart from a few years in]
War and a period of national servi
a tourist guide for many years, D
the ministry in the Church of England and took charge of the Saint
Michael-on-the-Mount Church in central Bristol in 1985.

Desmond retired at the age of sixty-five in 1994 and now lives
in Redland.

Bedminster Boy

DESMOND TUCKER

SilverWood

Published in 2017 by SilverWood Books

SilverWood Books Ltd
14 Small Street, Bristol, BS1 1DE, United Kingdom
www.silverwoodbooks.co.uk

Text and images © Desmond Tucker 2017

ISBN 978-1-78132-620-6 (paperback)
ISBN 978-1-78132-621-3 (ebook)

British Library Cataloguing in Publication Data
A CIP catalogue record for this book is available from
the British Library

Page design and typesetting by SilverWood Books
Printed on responsibly sourced paper

This book is dedicated to my parents pictured below, who gave me such a wonderful start in life, and to my brother Norman (4 years my junior) with whom I was always close until he died

Author's Note

Bedminster Boy was actually written by accident. My companion, Shazdeh (Farid Nikbakht), who is an Iranian-British citizen, used to listen to stories of my life and suggested that I should get them down in writing. Once they were written, he insisted that I should try to get this autobiography published.

Pam Dix, who is an elder at Stapleton Road Congregational Church, read the book after it was completed, typed it up for me and I sent the typed manuscript to SilverWood Books, who wrote to me and said they would love to publish it. The rest is history!

One

The Early Years

I was born February 18th 1929.

At that time my parents were in rooms at 26 Lime Road, Ashton Gate, Bristol. My mother's eldest sister and husband were in basement rooms at 44 Vicarage Road quite nearby. In those days most births took place at home with a midwife and doctor in attendance but it was decided that I should be born at Vicarage Road so that my Aunt Vera could take care of my mother during the confinement period. I have been told that when my mother began labour she and my father went round to Aunt Vera's where I was born in the front room in the basement. Incidentally, the weather was bitterly cold with ice and snow everywhere.

Many years later in the 1970s, one of my family invited me to a supper party in a basement flat in Vicarage Road, and to my amazement it was in the very house where I had been born, and even more strangely, the party took place in the room in which I had been born.

In 1931 we moved to a new council house at 11 Lynton Road just off St John's Lane, Bedminster, but I have memories of life in Lime Road despite being less than two years old when we left. I remember being taken by my mother to a friend's house in nearby Gaythorne

Road to hear my first radio. It was made of a plywood baffle board and was about three feet square with a loudspeaker set in it, and I believe the reception was from a crystal set.

The contraption was suspended from the picture rail and the reception was very erratic. You could intermittently hear voices or music between long periods of oscillation and interference, but nevertheless to everyone in the room it was quite miraculous. Mother's younger sister was married to Uncle Harry and he owned a crystal set, which did not have a loudspeaker and could only be heard by one person using headphones, and I can remember listening to that.

Another memory I have from the same period is being prepared to be taken out and sat on a rug while mother finished getting herself ready. Somehow I crawled to a cupboard and got out some black shoe polish and covered myself in it. I can also remember riding a small red tricycle through the passageway at my Aunt Vera's flat in Vicarage Road. My mother used to sing me lullabies when I was a baby and one of them was 'Go To Sleep, My Baby' and the other was 'When it's Springtime in the Rockies'. In later years when I mentioned this to my mother and sang the tunes she was amazed because I must have been a baby when she sang these songs to me.

Mother was inclined to be a bit hare-brained, and my father loved to tell a story which greatly embarrassed her. Apparently she took me out in my pram for the first time and went into a chemist, where she left me outside and returned home without me. When father asked, "Where's the baby?" she said, "Oh no, I've left him outside the chemist." She rushed back and found me unharmed and I accused her in later years of trying to dump me!

When we moved to Lynton Road it was part of a new estate and beyond the bottom of the garden were fields with cows and a farm nearby, but within five years a large school was constructed and the rest of the farm was swallowed up by new houses. Mother relied on Vera as her eldest sister so I saw a great deal of her; she often visited us and vice versa. I liked her very much, she was great fun and highly entertaining. She was also a very good organiser so as a result of her enterprising nature we often visited Bristol Zoo and had picnics in the nearby countryside and parks.

I remember she had a false tooth, and when I was naughty she would allow it to drop and it terrified me and I would say,'I'll be a good boy, Auntie Vera." She also told me of a fictitious friend whom she called Angelina Victoria, who she said could breathe fire just like a dragon on naughty boys. One day I was out with her and she stopped and spoke to a very imposing woman. After they parted she told me that the lady was Angelina Victoria, and I suppose in these days of psychoanalysis etc. any problems or maladjustments I suffered from in later life would be attributed to Aunt Vera's false tooth and Angelina Victoria!

Vera's husband Fred was also very fond of me and I remember him making me a sailing boat, which we sailed in the boating lake at Weston-super-Mare. Their oldest daughter Mona and I were almost the same age and we got on very well together. Vera and Fred moved from their basement flat in Vicarage Road to rented accommodation in Avonleigh Road, which was the next street to Hengaston Street where my grandmother on Mum's side lived with her youngest daughter Kate.

Both houses were on a Victorian estate called the Chessels, which wasn't far from Ashton Park. This is where Mona and I would go to play when Mum visited Vera. There were no private cars in those days so all the side roads were free of traffic and quite safe for children to play street games. If you walked along any of these streets you would see children playing marbles in the gutter, or whips and tops or hopscotch, and there was also a season for handstands.

There was also a game called pinny pop show. The idea of the game was for a child to get rid of unwanted toys like marbles or cigarette cards. They would set up a stall on the pavement and spread out all the things they wished to dispose of and sing, "Pinny pinny poppy show, who will come and have a go? Button or a pin." So if you were lucky you would gradually dispose of your wares in exchange for buttons or pins.

Another feature of street life was that in each street there were neighbours who would make toffee apples and toffee and coconut ice in their back kitchens and sell these items from their back doors to local children. We also liked to play mothers and fathers. You would lay out a pattern of bricks in the back yard to represent a house; someone would be the father and someone the mother. The game would involve dolls, live pets and kids of all ages acting out their home lives. If you were very lucky your mother might lend you her clothes horse, which you would cover with material to create a tent.

The greatest treat would be if Mother cooked a meal and bought it into the tent. Some very lucky children had a swing or seesaw in the garden. In our back garden we had a henhouse in which Mum raised chickens to sell for Christmas, which paid for our toys and presents. During the summer this shed was empty and we were allowed to turn it into a pirate ship called the Jolly Roger. Father even made a flagpole from which we flew a teacloth, which was supposed to be the *Jolly Roger* pirate flag.

The streets were full of life; there were no supermarkets but everything was delivered to your house and there would be daily visits from the milkman with a horse and cart and large churns of milk, which was measured into jugs for the housewives. There was also a baker's van, a fishmonger's, a coalman and occasionally a knife and scissors grinder. At different times of the day an ice cream van would appear and sometimes a tricycle selling Wall's ice cream. The slogan was 'Stop me and buy one'. Many years later I visited a gents' toilet which had the inevitable condom machine on the wall, and written on it was a parody of the Wall's slogan that said, 'Buy me and stop one!' This machine also dispensed condoms which had extra sensitivity. On the front of the machine there was an illustration which I have to admit looked like a Pope's tiara. Some wag had written underneath, 'As prescribed to the Pope'.

However, to return to the street vendors; there was also a fish and chip van which made visits on winter evenings. Of course when the housewives went out to purchase anything from the vendors there was a lot of gossip and social interchange as well as occasional street rows. I even remember the housewives fighting one another, and the whole street turned out to witness the spectacle and cheer on their favoured combatant.

Every street had a 'First-Aid Florrie' who always knew what to do with cuts and bruises or any other injury. There was also someone who would lay out corpses when anyone died. I remember seamstresses who would turn a ladies' two-piece into trousers; they were a godsend because often that was the only way we children could obtain clothes. Occasionally street outings would be organised and we would all go to Weston for the day.

The downside of today's life is that despite better housing, health conditions and living longer lives, because our entertainment is private and our lives are more private we've inevitably lost the feeling of community, which was once so strong. Even with travel, nearly everyone has a car and can get from A to B without meeting anyone. The modern supermarket is also so impersonal: I can remember visits to the shops with my mother to buy meat or groceries and there were always long discussions about cuts of bacon and the thickness of slices, tasting a bit of cheese before purchasing and meeting and chatting with other customers in the shops.

I particularly loved the Co-op because they had a system of overhead wires which conveyed small cylindrical containers, into which were placed the bill and the cash for purchases which the customer had made. The container was clipped to the wire, a lever was pulled and then the contraption sped across the tight overhead wire to an office where a girl checked out the bill and money and returned the cylinder in the same way to the shop assistant who had sent it. If you were a Co-op member it would also contain dividend tokens and milk tokens. It really fascinated me to see all these wooden cylinders whizzing across the shop ceiling via high wires.

One day when we visited Auntie Vera, Mona and I were allowed to go to Ashton Park where we found some blackberry bushes laden with fruit. We began picking some of the berries and eating them, and then decided it would be a good idea to take some home for our mums. Mona was wearing a dress with pockets in the front, which we packed with the ripe blackberries, and I filled my trouser pockets. Of course the juice ran out everywhere and when we got home we were lifted up to see our faces reflected in the mirror absolutely covered with the juice; it had also run from my pockets and down my legs and the same had happened to Mona. Both of us cried but we were not punished as our mums were hysterical with laughing about it all. I saw a lot of Mona until she married and I must admit we always seemed to be getting involved in escapades.

Life at Lynton Road between 1931 and 1939 was good on both a family level and a personal one, but Mum and Dad were very worried about world events from the time that Mussolini sent his army into Abyssinia. Then of course there was the rise to power of Hitler and the Nazis in Germany. Although neither of my parents talked to me directly about their worries, I heard enough snatches of conversation to be worried myself.

I used to like to visit my Auntie Kate because she was never too busy to bother with me. Inevitably she would offer to take me 'down Bedminster'. All Bedminster people loved East Street, which we all referred to as 'Bemmy'. In pre-war days it was a wonderland of marvellous shops, which sold everything and stretched all the way from Bedminster Bridge to the London Inn. Auntie Kate would take me to Bedminster Bridge on a tram, one of a very large fleet which covered all of Bristol.

During the wartime blitzes the main power station at Counterslip was permanently put out of action by the bombing, as was the Bedminster tram depot, which was at the top of Sheen Road opposite what is now Cameron's Balloon Factory. The trams had open tops and could be driven from either end. Another innovation was that they had scoop trays at either end so that if any animal or person fell in front of a tram they would not fall under the wheels, but be scooped up into the scoop tray.

There is another story which, although not directly linked to my life story, I would nevertheless like to tell. During the '30s a fascist party known as the Blackshirts made many bids for power, led by Sir Oswald Mosley. They were generally disliked by all but persisted in holding rallies, usually in working class areas like Bedminster. One such rally was held at the bottom of the street known as The Nursery, where it joined North Street. It was a street where you would often see women with caps on sitting on their front doorsteps smoking their pipes. However, the speaker at this rally stood in front of a house on a box and used a loudhailer. The police had commandeered a tram and were all waiting inside it, anticipating trouble.

Anyway, a little old lady appeared at the bedroom window holding an empty chamber pot and carefully took aim. When the positioning was just right she dropped the pot on to the speaker's head. There was absolute pandemonium as he was knocked unconscious. The police dived into the crowd and most of the man's followers were bundled into the tram and driven to Bedminster police station; it was like something from a Keystone Cops film! I remember about thirty to forty years after this event a slogan could still be seen painted in large white letters on a brick wall in Sheen Road. It proclaimed, 'Mosley will win', but someone had altered it to read, 'Mosley will swing'.

Auntie Kate would take me on the tram to Bedminster Bridge; then we would walk back through Bedminster and she would give me sixpence to spend. In those days sixpence would go quite a long way, in fact Woolworth's advertised itself as a threepenny and sixpenny store; I suppose today's equivalent is Poundstretcher. There used to be a theatre in East Street, Bedminster known as the Bedminster Hippodrome, which originally opened as a variety theatre, but in those early days of movie films it was turned into a cinema and became known as the Stoll Picture House. The films were all silent to begin with, but then sound was added and these films were known as talkies. For some years both types of films were shown, but gradually the talkies took over.

There was a girl in our street called Doreen Long, who liked taking neighbours' children out, and she took me to the Stoll to see *Alice in Wonderland*, which was a silent picture, and this was my very first visit to the cinema. The Stoll was very smart. There was a flight of steps leading up to the entrance and there was always a commissionaire outside in a very smart uniform, peaked cap and white gloves, to welcome patrons. A feature of this cinema was that if you sat in the very best seats, in the afternoon you could order and pay for tea when you went in, and it would be brought to your seat in the interval.

Another happy memory I have of the '30s is the annual visit to the pantomime at the Prince's Theatre, and as usual Auntie Vera was the organiser. This theatre stood between Park Street and Park Row. Its pantomimes were famous for spectacular scenery and of course there was the principal boy, played by a woman, and a pantomime dame played by a man. There was usually a demon that shot up through a trap door on to the stage, and a flying ballet dancer suspended on fine wires above the auditorium.

There were many other traditions including a community song for the audience. A huge song sheet was suspended in front of the stage with the words in very large letters. One of the comics would teach us the tune and then the audience would be divided into sections, such as the gallery, the grand circle, the boxes and the pit, and then we would all have to compete to see who could sing the best. There was also a scene where the pantomime dame got ready for bed and undressed behind a screen. She threw her clothes over the screen and there would be piles of outrageous underwear. We were encouraged to boo the villain and cheer the heroine. Mother and Auntie Vera would fill carrier bags with goodies and we would queue up for cheap seats in the gallery. Looking back it was two and a half to three hours of sheer pleasure and excitement. Sadly the Prince's Theatre was destroyed in the Bristol blitzes.

Auntie Vera and Uncle Fred always threw a party for all the children of the family at Christmas, which they held in their front room. There was a piano and Auntie Vera could play, so there were songs and games and presents from the Christmas tree. If we paid them a visit in the evening, Uncle Fred would be sent out to a nearby fish and chip shop for our supper. It was called The Little Wonder and it stood in West Street.

There were also visits to the zoo, which included a ride on the elephant and meeting Alfred the gorilla, and to Weston-super-Mare. In those days there were many more stalls on the beach than there are today. There was a famous fish and chip shop in the town called Coffins and someone would bring us fish and chips to eat on the beach; one of the stalls sold jugs of tea complete with cups and saucers on a tray, and to make sure it was all returned a deposit had to be paid at the time of purchase. There was also an open-air variety theatre on the beach. The stage was covered by a canvas awning and there was an enclosure in front of it, for which you had to pay for a ticket for entry, and there were deckchairs inside but it was all surrounded by chestnut paling so you could stand outside and see the show for free. The company was called the Troubador Follies.

A Professor Staddon also had a Punch and Judy show on the beach, and there were donkey rides. So with all these things and a swimming pool opened in the mid '30s, two model yacht ponds and the pier, there was plenty to do in addition to the building of sandcastles and paddling if the tide was in. It was the only time I got to travel on a train and that alone was very exciting.

I was very fond of my granddad. He was a very short man with a large moustache; however one thing I didn't like was that when we visited him at his home in Temple Street, he always kissed me when I left and the bristles of his moustache tickled my face. His two daughters, Dora and Elsie, his son Frank and Dora's daughter lived with him.

Dad had another sister, Lill, and two brothers, Fred and Wally. Lill was the eldest, and because Dad's mother had died in the flu epidemic of 1918, she had brought up the family. She in turn had a large family of her own, and they lived at 82 Lynton Road. Dad also had a spinster aunt called Salina, who lived in Sion Road and had a lodger called Victor; we were regularly taken to visit her but I dreaded those visits for two reasons: one, we were always taken into her front room, which was full of Victorian furniture with the inevitable aspidistra in the window and horsehair chairs which tickled the backs of your legs when you sat on them, and two, we were always offered a slice of seed cake, which I hated but out of courtesy dared not refuse! Incidentally, Auntie Lill had lived in London during the 1914 war and could remember the Zeppelin raids.

The first school I attended at the age of five was Parsons Street Infants School, and oddly enough my grandfather was the foreman of the works when it was built in 1908. The headmistress in my time was Miss Alexander, who had been the headmistress when my father attended the school. Her brother was the first lord of the admiralty. Although it wasn't a church school we always met in the hall for a daily service where there was a daily Scripture reading, after the registers had been called. We were all recommended to drink a third of a pint of milk a day, which was available for free to the less well-off children.

There were regular health checks and head inspections to see if we were harbouring fleas or lice. We were also regularly checked for rickets or other signs of vitamin deficiency. I can remember being put on a course of Parrish's chemical food, which was foul, and cod liver oil and malt, which was like a gooey toffee. Of course there was no National Health Service but for those considered too poor to pay for medicine there were free dispensaries. One was in Mill Lane, Bedminster, and we collected medication from there.

The first children's health clinic opened at the junction of Dean Road and Warden Road, opposite a bicycle shop run by a man we all knew as Chinny Pope. His shop sign was a penny-farthing bike fixed to the wall above the window. The clinic was in a private house. This clinic played a big part in our school lives; impetigo, a nasty infectious skin disease, was rife in the schools and had to be treated at the clinic. A mauve-coloured lotion was painted on the skin (I wonder whether it was permanganate of potash), which was very embarrassing because the dye persisted for days until the infection was cured. My mother always dashed up to the school and demanded to know, "Why has my Desmond caught this again?" She was told that the cleaner the child is, the more prone they are to this kind of infection! We all seemed to catch the measles, mumps and whooping cough, and some children caught diphtheria, scarlet fever, and one or two had polio. I was OK with measles but had bronchitis with whooping cough and had septic glands with mumps; the treatment was hot poultices applied to the affected glands.

Uncle Harry had a butcher's van and used to deliver meat in our street. During our summer holiday he turned up one day and announced he was taking us to Burnham-on-Sea in his van. Mum was not keen for us to go but Harry would have none of it.

"Come on, Tuck, don't bugger about, get the boys ready and let's be off." I think Mother was thinking that if his driving was anything like his lifestyle it would be a very erratic, hair-raising and bumpy ride. Anyway, we were all bundled into the van where Auntie Vera and her two daughters, Mona and Heather, were sitting on the floor looking as though they had been kidnapped. We sped away at breakneck speed and I can still remember the smell of stale meat. The inside of the van was like an oven and I think most of us were sick. Give Uncle Harry his due, once he got us to Burnham, he gave us all a marvellous time and was generous to a fault.

He always managed to throw a New Year's party for the family at 26 Hengaston Street. It was anything but a genteel affair. He managed to get hold of a barrel of beer and the lino in the hall was floating on spilt ale. My grandmother was a very good pianist and provided she was plied with enough beer she would play like a concert pianist. Of Harry she always said, "That man is a blaggard." Nevertheless she played for hours and we all sang. As midnight approached Harry grabbed the tin bath and led us out into the street! The noise was deafening.

My mother was educated at Luckwell Road School. A friend of hers lived on a farm at the end of South Liberty Lane, so another treat for us was to visit this farm for a picnic in one of the fields;

oddly enough the farmhouse still survives. It is quite near the main railway line but is now swamped by industrial buildings and is used as offices.

In the 1930s Whitchurch was the site of Bristol Airport and was about three miles from our house in Lynton Road. To get to it we walked up to the end of the street, went up Novers Hill Lane and continued along the deserted country lanes until we reached the airport. Quite often during the summer holiday Mum packed bread and jam and homemade lemonade for my brother Norman and me, and we would then walk to the airport to sit by the boundary fence and watch the planes taking off and landing.

They were biplanes with large windows, through which we could see the wealthy passengers. The taxiing point was so near the fence that we could wave to the passengers and they would wave back. Eventually when the 1939 war began, Imperial Airways, as the national line was called, moved from London to Bristol and our airport became quite important. Ilchester Crescent at Bedminster Down was built to accommodate the staff who had transferred here from London.

The 1930s were a pioneering time for air travel and at that time there were no commercial airlines between the UK and USA, so to promote air travel regular air displays were held annually at most British airports, and Norman and I used to go to Whitchurch to watch the spectacular displays. To hear a plane fly overhead at that time was such a rarity that children in the streets would shout, "Aeroplane!" and everyone would rush out to see it fly over. When Norman and I returned home we always stopped at the Pigeon House Stream, near where the huge Hartcliffe cigarette factory was eventually built in the 1970s, where we would fish for minnows to take home in jam jars.

Apart from sailing to the US in a liner, which took approximately seven days, the only viable way of getting there was by airship, which could travel twice as fast as the liners. I remember seeing the R101 fly over our house. It was an amazing sight; just like a huge silver cigar floating in the sky. The big drawback with these flying monsters was that they were packed in the main body of the ship with huge balloons filled with hydrogen, which was highly inflammable and thus gave them the power to lift. I think the R101 crashed into a hillside in France, and the German Zeppelin exploded on landing in the USA. So that was the end of airship travel.

Soon after we moved to Lynton Road a mission church was built to serve the housing estate. It was Anglican and was dedicated to St Hugh of Lincoln. It was the first dual-purpose place of worship to be built in Bristol, and was a bit of a novelty. It was simply an oblong building divided into three rooms at its east end. On the left as you faced east there was a kitchen, which doubled up as a choir vestry on Sundays. On the right was the clergy vestry. The centre space, about fourteen feet square, was the sanctuary and it opened out into the hall. On weekdays a large wooden roller shutter could be pulled down to shut it off and convert the nave into a hall.

I was sent to the church quite soon after it opened in 1931. There was a very large Sunday school but I think there were two reasons for the large numbers: one was that if you attended regularly you could obtain a free train ticket once a year for an outing to Weston-super-Mare with free tea thrown in, and two, in those days most employers demanded a good Sunday school reference to offer you a job.

Although my parents did not become involved with churchgoing until 1938, nevertheless my mother taught me to say evening prayers and read the Bible to me. I suppose this set me out on a journey through life which would involve the Christian faith. When I was ten years old in 1939 my mother gave me my first Bible, which I still have. Mother was conditionally baptised and then confirmed in 1938. A large part of this was due to the influence of Sister Vincent from the convent in Redcatch Road, who rented our box room as an office and base, from which she worked in the parish each day.

Another strong influence was Minnie Gallery who lived with her mother and her husband Joe in Wingfield Road. She sponsored my mother, both for her baptism and confirmation, and they were good friends. Her husband Joe had been an officer in the Royal Navy during the 1914–18 war He was retired by the time they came to Bristol in the '30s, but joined the Royal Navy volunteer reserves and was captain of *HMS Flying Fox*, which was an old Corvette that been converted into a training ship and was moored by the Mardyke Ferry in Bristol Docks. We often visited the ship as Joe's guests. Minnie's mother was a lovely old lady with a strong cockney accent and dressed in Victorian clothes. She was very jolly and I think I felt more of an affinity with her than my own grandmother.

I am the oldest in the family and have three younger brothers and no sisters. I was born February 18th 1929 and my next brother, Norman, was born January 26th 1933. Then there was quite a long gap before the next two were born April 28th 1942 and November 2nd 1946 respectively. So with the long gap between myself and the last two, we were almost like two families. We all got on well as brothers but the next eldest was especially close to me. This is probably due to the 1939–46 war, because so much of the world that Norman and I knew changed radically during that war. The pre-war years had been such a huge part of our lives, as had some of the traumatic wartime experiences, so we had common ground to share for the rest of our lives. Although my second-youngest brother was born in the middle of an air raid at Clevedon and the youngest at Bristol Maternity Hospital, their shared experience was from the late '40s so any knowledge they had of the war and its devastating effect on Britain was second-hand. Norman and I remained close and in regular contact with each other until he died from a severe stroke, and I have to admit I am still missing him terribly.

When I attended Parsons Street Junior School we had a teacher called Miss Millard, and for our literature class she read *The Wind in the Willows* to us and it has remained my favourite book ever since. My parents were by no means intellectuals but they encouraged me to read and write from a very early age. One Christmas the main present from them was a book called *The Children's Golden Treasury*, but to really appreciate this you had to be able to read so this provided a natural incentive to read and write.

The 1930s saw a great period for building luxury cinemas in Bedminster. Before this period there were, in addition to the Stoll Picture House, two cinemas, or fleapits as they were known. One was the Town Hall in Canon Street and the other was the Ashton Cinema, which stood at the junction of Raleigh Road and North Street. I remember that the auxiliary lighting in the town hall was gas, and the only usher was a man of middle age who always wore a cap and kept order.

If there was any untoward behaviour he would shout in a strong Bristol accent, "Shut thee bloody nise", which translated into English was, 'Shut your bloody noise.'

Another peculiarity of these fleapits was that the lighting for the projectors was a carbon flame, which had a tendency to break down. It began by making the screen go an odd violet colour; then there would be a complete blackout, but the audience loved this and would shout and whistle until the projectionist fitted a new carbon and the film continued.

I rarely went to the Ashton Cinema but I do know that the roof leaked and if you sat upstairs you needed to dodge the raindrops. Anyway, Bedminster's first luxury cinema was the Ambassador, which was built on the site of an old clay pit at the junction of Winterstoke and Luckwell Road. The story goes that a Bedminster entrepreneur visited the US and saw a spectacular cinema and was so impressed that he managed to obtain a set of plans for it, and paid for the construction of the Ambassador Cinema on the site of the old disused clay pit, which he owned, using the plans from the USA. The result was a truly magnificent example of Art Deco.

Mother always took me to see Shirley Temple films – Shirley was a Hollywood child prodigy, but I shall never forget the unashamed luxury of the Ambassador. At home we had bare lino in the rooms but at this cinema you seemed to almost wade through deep pile carpets. There were also smart usherettes who showed you to your seats, and because it was before aerosols were invented, attendants passed up and down the aisles pumping perfume into the air.

All the lighting was carefully concealed and during the interval the stage was flooded with an ever-changing display of coloured lights. Altogether it was an escape into Hollywood glamour, and during the '30s similar cinemas were being opened all over Britain. Sadly all this came to an end in the '60s with the increased popularity of TV, and also with the rising teenage cult increasing unruly behaviour in cinemas and public places.

A very large influence in my life in the 1930s was my attendance at St Hugh's Mission Church in Lynton Road. The mother church was St John the Baptist in Bedminster, which pioneered the Oxford Movement in Bedminster during the nineteenth century, so both churches were Anglo-Catholic with a great deal of elaborate ritual. They were both served by a staff of celibate priests who were based at Kelham in Yorkshire, and they were assisted by a staff of nuns who belonged to the Order of St Vincent De Paul and were based in a convent in Redcatch Road, Knowle. The nuns rented rooms in our locality and used them as offices and teaching bases, so they actually lived and slept at the convent but rented rooms during the day.

The religious instruction in the parish was very thorough and I learned a lot from it. There was, in addition to a very large Sunday school, a Scout troop with Scouts, Cubs, Guides and Brownies. Sadly the downside of all this was that we were indoctrinated with a very strong sense of guilt about our potential wickedness. For example, I was given a so-called children's prayer book which advocated sacramental confession to a priest, and when I made my first confession at the age of nine I looked up sins in this book, some of which I didn't have the foggiest understanding of, especially those concerning sexual misdemeanours.

Great emphasis was placed on our creator being a God of judgement and wrath, who sooner or later would judge and condemn us if we did not come up to His exacting standards. In retrospect I think the underlying purpose behind this doctrine was to frighten gullible people into behaving in a suitable way to make them worthy to enter the Kingdom of Heaven. This is a complete contradiction to what I have wrestled with about the doctrine of divine grace, by which we can never earn or deserve by our own effort a place in the Kingdom of Heaven. An example of this kind of attitude is typified by a thing I recall from the 1930s.

One of our neighbours at Lynton Road lost her firstborn son in infancy and one of the nuns paid her a visit and discovered that the child was not baptised, and irrespective of the woman being in the first stages of grief, the nun made it her business to tell this woman that because her son had not been baptised God would bar him from Heaven and therefore she would never meet him again.

So much for a compassionate and loving God! This is not a personal gripe on my part against the staff of St Hugh's or St John's because sadly at that time Christian teaching was largely orientated in that way and must have contributed to the dwindling number of church members.

As I matured into adulthood I found I could not get my head around the idea of God being both a loving God, as depicted by the prodigal son parable and the willingness of Jesus to love and accept all people in such an open way, and the God of wrath and judgement that I had been taught about in my childhood. Finally this dilemma led me to break all my ties with the church for about twenty years, although I continued to say my prayers and still regarded it as an obligation to make my communion on Easter Sunday.

During the mid 1930s the country celebrated the silver jubilee of King George V and all of us schoolchildren were given commemorative china mugs, and then in 1935 the king died and Edward, Prince of Wales was proclaimed king. He was due to be crowned in 1936 and once again we were all given commemorative mugs for his coronation. It turned out, however, that he was courting an American divorcee called Mrs Wallis Simpson, and of course in those days it was considered unthinkable that a divorcee could become queen consort. Edward was given an option that he could marry Mrs Simpson and still be crowned king, but she could not become queen. This he refused to accept and abdicated and took the title of Duke of Windsor, and she became Duchess of Windsor.

His younger brother had to take his place and took the title of George VI, which was something neither he nor his wife wanted because he had a bad stutter. Nevertheless his coronation took place in 1937 and he became a brilliant wartime leader, much loved and respected by everyone. But this awesome task took its toll and he died of lung cancer in 1952. Incidentally, we children were given yet another commemorative mug for his coronation.

Two events stick with me from the 1930s: first, a neighbour in Temple Street, Bedminster, where my father spent much of his childhood, asked Dad if he would like a parrot and I watched the bird eating and observed that it liked sunflower seeds and red chillies, so I thought I would try it. I put a chilli in my mouth and of course it was extremely hot. I couldn't speak and I rushed into the kitchen and flooded my mouth with cold water to try and stop the burning. The sensation was so hot I couldn't speak. Mother asked what the matter was and I couldn't even reply, but panted frantically.

The second event was when Mother fell down in the living room and broke her tibia. My father rushed out and shouted for help. She had to be taken to the Bristol Royal Infirmary where they put her leg in splints; then the following day they set it in plaster of Paris right up to her thigh. I have been told that the BRI was the first hospital in the country to set broken limbs with plaster of Paris and give patients a degree of mobility.

A few weeks after this accident my father's sister Elsie died at the age of thirty with a heart attack, and hers was a horse-drawn funeral. Not only was the hearse horse-drawn, but also the carriages for the mourners. Of course, seeing as my mother was plastered from her ankle to her thigh for six weeks and could not get into the carriage, she was unable to attend the funeral. I remember the horse-drawn funerals from that period very well.

Two

The 1939–45 War Air Raids

By 1938 war with Germany became inevitable and preparation for it began in earnest. Many public buildings had protective walls of sandbags built outside their entrances and all of us were issued with gas masks, which were carried everywhere in cardboard boxes. Quite often we would do some lessons wearing them. Basically they were rubber masks with a filtering snout at the front through which purified air was admitted, but when the wearer breathed out the air was expelled through the sides of the mask. To our delight, we children discovered that if you blew hard enough you could produce a loud noise like a horse farting! Imagine a class full of children making these awful noises like a demonic choir. It must have driven the teachers mad.

It was also compulsory for everyone to possess, and to carry at all times, an identity card. This was in anticipation of bombing as a means of identifying bodies. Air raid posts were constructed as the centres of operations in the event of air raids. A militia force was formed to train civilians for military service and an auxiliary fire brigade was formed to fight fires, which my father joined. Homes which had gardens were supplied on request with Anderson shelters made of strong corrugated steel, which could be built in a hole about three feet deep in the garden and below ground level, and were lined with concrete. Each shelter could accommodate two families and they were reckoned to be blast-proof. Where people lived in flats or an Anderson shelter could not be fitted, they were supplied with a Morrison shelter, which was literally a reinforced steel table beneath which a family could shelter. The only other alternative which was considered to be comparatively safe was the cupboard under the stairs. So with all the preparation going on there was an awful sense of foreboding about what was likely to happen, but as far as possible life went on as normal.

At the beginning of 1939 the RAF moved into wired-off areas in the open spaces of the cities and set up balloon sites. The idea being that the balloons, which were about thirty to forty feet long, filled with hydrogen or helium and attached to flexible cables on a coil, could be sent up into the sky to a height of over five hundred feet and it was believed that the vertical networks of wire would be a deterrent to dive-bombers. The downside was that the balloons and wires proved to be perfect lightning conductors during thunderstorms, but I loved to see the balloons get struck by lightning and come down in balls of flame.

Final futile gestures were made to Germany but the spark that finally caused the outbreak of war in September 1939 was a small corridor of land belonging to Poland, which was their only access to open sea and known as the Polish Corridor. The Germans threatened to invade this piece of land and the British government warned them that if their plans went ahead a state of war would exist between us and them. They chose to ignore this warning and were given a deadline of 11am on September 3rd, so at that time war broke out.

Nothing dramatic happened at first, although a British expeditionary force was sent to Europe while the Germans remorselessly overran and conquered all the countries around them. I was old enough to listen to and understand the newscasts about this. A series of nuisance raids started in Bristol and we spent many nights out in the shelter and nothing happened, but in the meantime the Battle of Britain was being fought out over the skies of Kent. Hermann

Goering, the head of the German air force, convinced Hitler that he could destroy the RAF and once this had happened, the invasion of Britain could go ahead and victory was around the corner for them. But he badly underestimated the skill and heroism of the few young British airmen and their Polish and Empire colleagues, who in their Spitfire and Hurricane fighter planes successfully fought the German air force.

Winston Churchill, our wartime Prime Minister, made a number of inspiring broadcasts that I well remember; he was a superb orator and leader and a master of the English language. Two of his speeches in particular I will never forget, one of which referred to the Battle of Britain pilots.

He said, "If the British Empire should last a thousand years, people will say that this was their finest hour." Yes! We truly had our backs to the wall and were fully aware of the danger but Winston's words inspired us all and gave us the determination to carry on.

By the autumn of 1940 Field Marshall Goering, the commander of the Luftwaffe, knew that the Germans had lost the Battle of Britain and convinced Hitler that their strategy was too costly in planes and manpower. So by the end of August the daylight raids ceased, but later in the year a relentless round of night raids or blitzes on our major cities began.

The system for educating children until the late 1940s was totally different from today. There was infant school, which you commenced at the age of five, then you transferred to junior school at the age of eight in which there were three streams, A, B and C; A being for the potentially brighter children. Then at the age of eleven everyone took a preliminary exam and those who passed sat for a scholarship exam, which determined the type of senior school you would attend. The downside of the system was that regardless of your previous experience at school your whole future was set entirely by the results of the preliminary and scholarship exams.

Since I was ordained in 1986 and became a chaplain to one of the private schools in Clifton, I learned how in these schools, children are totally focused on the techniques of passing exams, something which in my pre-war schooling I was taught nothing about. Consequently, on the crucial day of my preliminary exam I completely panicked, with disastrous results, and failed the exam. Children in my situation went on to an elementary school and were groomed for manual work, or in the case of girls maybe for shop work. So in a way we were, because of a bad performance on the crucial exam day, doomed to some kind of manual work or inferior jobs. Thank God that grossly unfair system was abolished and replaced by something better!

Before the war my mother worked cleaning solicitors' offices in Unity Street just behind the Bristol Hippodrome. These offices were old Georgian houses three storeys high. Her job, as well as cleaning, was to lay the coal fires and carry buckets of coal to the upper floors. To do this she commenced work at 6am. Dad began work at Rowe Brothers in Canons Marsh much later, so he got Norman and me out of bed, gave us our breakfast and prepared us for school. Then when he left for work he locked the sitting room door and left by the front door and we sat in the kitchen until it was time for us to go to school. Looking back at those days it must have been a hard life for Mum and Dad to earn enough money to keep a roof over our heads.

Saturday morning was always a treat for Norman and me because we took a bus to the centre of town and waited for Mum to finish work by about 10am. It was very interesting because at that time the harbour extended to Baldwin Street so St Augustine's Quay outside the Hippodrome really was a true quay, with ships tied up, loading and unloading cargo. It wasn't until about 1938 that the builders began piledriving to cover the water and create what has now become a kind of piazza. When Mum finished work she met us and took us to Castle Street, which was then Bristol's main shopping area, and buy us a treat.

I suppose my parents' only luxury was that in the evening they put us both to bed by 9pm and then she prepared supper for them both. They would put the radio on and listen to dance music, which was broadcast by the BBC from one of London's nightclubs. I think their favourite bands were Henry Hall's and Ambrose's; we liked lying in bed and listening to the music.

In the first few months of the war nothing much happened because, despite rationing, other restrictions and practising for air raids and gas attacks, life in our part of the world remained unbelievably normal. There were exceptions, however. I remember I was in Victoria Park, Bedminster, during a lovely summer day in 1940 and the air raid sirens sounded. Then suddenly the sky was filled with German aircraft that were bombing the Filton Aircraft Factory. I was absolutely fascinated by the blobs of smoke caused by the gunfire and the air display. Then an air raid warden grabbed me and bundled me into an air raid shelter. We learned hundreds of aircraft workers had been killed at Filton that day.

Sunday November 24th was a perfect evening with a clear sky and full moon. Norman and I had been sent to church for the 6.30pm evensong at St Hughes. Mother told us later that as she journeyed to see her mother at Bedminster Down Road, lots of German planes flew over and lit up the sky with flares and she said it became like daylight. Our service in church continued with us at first unaware of what was happening outside because the church, in common with all properties, had blackout material over the windows. Then as the service proceeded the gunfire became louder by the minute and bombs began to fall. It became so noisy that the service was abandoned and we gathered around the piano singing hymns and ducking as the bombs fell.

Father came to fetch us and take us home and the sight that greeted us when we left the church was awe-inspiring and terrifying. From the direction of the city the sky was one mass of flames and smoke, and even in Lynton Road you could smell the burning and ashes were falling like a snowstorm. Bombs were dropping and shrapnel from gunfire was pinging down. Father had his fireman's helmet and gas mask with him and he put the helmet on Norman and the gas mask pack on my head. He gathered us close to him and ordered us to drop down to the ground if he shouted, "Down." We reached home and went to the Anderson shelter, where our neighbours from number 13 were waiting. This was about 7pm and from then till midnight, until the all-clear was given, all Hell was let loose.

With a major blitz (as the raids were known), there was a manic routine; the bombers were not overhead all the time but seemed to fly over in waves, so there were short periods of comparative calm. Then you could hear the next flight of bombers approaching and the bombs getting closer. You seemed to instinctively know when to position yourself safely, e.g. mouth shut tight, breathe out and put fingers in ears – It is very strange, but after a few hours you became used to it and almost too fed up to be terrified.

About midnight the all-clear was sounded and we came out of the shelter to discover our house had been hit. Our house, number 11, was one of a pair of semi-detached houses, the other being number 13. I think that the bomb that hit ours must have been quite small because it only made a three-foot crater in the rear garden. What seems to have happened is that it hit the corner of the rear of the house and the impact tore away the corner and much of the back upstairs and downstairs wall, leaving the bathroom, bedroom and kitchen with most of the wall ripped off. Then it exploded in the garden and pushed the whole house forward on its foundations. The parrot was still in its cage in the living room quite unharmed, but of course the house was uninhabitable and irreparable. The odd thing is that in a later raid number 13 took a direct hit and was completely demolished and the demolition squad came and pulled down the ruins of our house.

The next problem was where to sleep, so we returned with Uncle Ewart to Bedminster Down and Aunt Ada made up temporary beds on the floor for us and we stayed there for a few days until Aunt Kate, who lived at number 23 Hengaston Street, offered us a couple of rooms. We were lucky that we had somewhere to go, but many bomb victims were housed and fed in public halls. There were places where people could get a bath and be kitted out with clothes, which were largely donated by our friends in the USA.

In Marksbury Road, before the war, there were two large gas-ometers which we all thought were full of coal gas but in fact they were full of water above a kind of diaphragm, below which was the gas, and the pressure of the water pushed the gas through the pipes to the consumers. Anyway, on November 24th one of these holders was hit by a large bomb and split open, causing many thousands of gallons of water to be released, which flooded the Anderson shelters in Marksbury Road where residents were sheltering. There was such a massive rush of water that many of the people sheltering below ground level were drowned.

Uncle Ewart had insisted on bringing my mother home, and as well as picking their way through debris and passing bombed houses and burning property, they saw bodies being brought out of the air raid shelters near the gas holders by rescue workers. When they turned the corner into Lynton Road they saw a crowd standing outside our house but the damage was to the back of the house; from a distance the front looked undamaged. Mother panicked because she assumed that something had happened to us. Someone in the crowd reassured her that we were all OK but that the back of the house had been badly damaged. Anyway, after moving to Auntie Kate's house we stayed there for six weeks, during which time the Blitz continued. In total Bristol had six major blitzes between November 24th and Good Friday 1941, and a total of just over 1,500 people were killed in these raids with many more injured.

The fire brigade became better organised so that if there was a blitz in a particular city all the fire brigades from a large area of the country converged on that city to help it fight the fires. The result was that we sometimes didn't see Father for many weeks. When he did come home he absolutely stank of burning and often just fell on to the sofa and slept with sheer exhaustion. We learned later that he went from Plymouth to Exeter and over to Cardiff without getting a rest.

That year, 1940, we did our best to celebrate Christmas, not just coping with rationing as everyone else was, but trying to live in two small rooms. One thing I do remember is that Mother bought me my first pair of long trousers. In those days most boys began to wear long trousers when they were about eleven years old and it's hard to imagine now but there were no such things as jeans in those days.

On the afternoon of January 2nd or 3rd we all went for a trip down to the tip just off St John's Lane to see an ARP demonstration of the best way to deal with an incendiary bomb. Those bombs were quite small, about fifteen inches long and two inches thick, and they were made of magnesium and aluminium, which detonated and burned with a very intense heat, like a giant firework. The ARP rigged up some huts that were open on one side and furnished like a room. Then they detonated a bomb by striking it nose down. It exploded quite easily and burned from the nose to the tail; then they threw the bomb into the hut and within a minute the fierce heat and flames destroyed everything.

When the war started we were issued with stirrup pumps to use on these bombs, but it was discovered that the oxygen which is present in water actually fed the flames and made the situation worse. Then they demonstrated another way of putting out these incendiary devices – it was to use dry sand or earth and smother the bomb with it, and it really was effective. It was also discovered that if you deployed people to fire-watch on roof sites, if they spotted an incendiary bomb burning, and if they were quick enough, they could grab the burning bomb by its fin and throw it from the roof on to the ground.

When we went home we put buckets of sand and a shovel at the top of our stairs! Ironically within a day or two this proved to be a futile exercise; on Friday January 3rd 1941 a major raid commenced at 6.30pm. We had a mattress to sit on in a cupboard underneath the stairs, and as was normal, Auntie Kate, her daughter Betty and six-month-old son Colin were joined by Mother, Norman and me and it was quite a tight squeeze in that cupboard. Anyway, the bombs started falling and judging by the loud explosions we knew that a much heavier kind of bomb was being used. The ferocity of the raid was worse than any previous one we had experienced, and on many occasions the roof shook so much that we thought it would collapse. This continued until midnight and we thought that the air raid had finished when the all-clear sounded.

We decided to stretch our legs and see how Auntie Vera and Uncle Fred and their two girls had fared. The damage everywhere was terrible and there were great lumps of rubble in the street, and most of the houses had smashed windows and roof tiles missing. I think we stayed at Aunt Vera's just long enough for a cup of tea; then another air raid warning sounded at 12.30pm. We would have liked to have stayed with them but their air raid shelter was already overcrowded so we headed home.

We walked we passed a street shelter; these were erected in the street all over the city and offered shelter to anyone caught in the open in the event of an air raid. They were made of thick brick walls with a solid concrete flat roof and had benches inside. We had half a mind not to return home but to shelter in this street shelter instead, but Mum remembered Dad warning her not to use that shelter as he said he had a bad feeling about it and she had promised that none of us would shelter there; so we went back to our shelter under the stairs. We found out later that the bomb that hit us had killed everyone in that street shelter! It was alongside a small coal yard and a couple of days later as I passed the yard, I saw the bodies of those poor people laid out in rows and covered in coal sacks.

During the raid in which we were bombed, a tram which was travelling through West Street was lifted up by the bomb blast and embedded in the front of a shop. I can also remember a few days after the raid, walking through West Street with my cousin Mona when a time bomb exploded beneath a greengrocer's shop. It was an oil bomb and within minutes the whole building was engulfed in flames. Luckily all the customers and the owner escaped before the fire really took hold.

On the night of November 24th our beloved church, St John's, Bedminster, was destroyed by fire together with St Paul's, Bedminster, and St Francis', Ashton Gate was also destroyed in another blitz.

I suppose in these days an army of counsellors would move in to counsel victims but in those days we were told that we were British and had to get on with it and not let it get us down! I must confess this experience has haunted me ever since and until quite recently I could not bear to watch anything on TV that brought these awful memories back to me, so writing this is not just getting my life story on paper, it is truly therapeutic. Nowadays when I see innocent people suffering bombing or having to flee their homeland I instinctively feel that, yes, in a small way I have been there!

Anyway, at 12.30 in the morning we arrived home and the bombing started all over again. Then at 2.20am there was an enormous explosion and the house collapsed around us; it was a terrifying experience. We were completely in the dark in the cupboard under the stairs with only a box of matches, which we lit to check that none of us were dead or injured. The strange thing is that as all this happened I prayed and put us all into the hands of God, and after all the debris had stopped falling and the dust settled, I felt a strange feeling that a presence was with us.

I can remember either Mum or Auntie Kate saying, "Well, we're stuck here and can't do anything about it, and another thing, lightning doesn't strike twice in the same place so we're safe now." The debris above muffled the noise of the raid and I think we all slept for a few hours.

From their front bedroom window Auntie Ada and Uncle Ewart had a grandstand view of the bombing, and when the one that hit us exploded Ada said to Ewart, "I'm sure that's Kate's house, we must get round there."

Ewart said, "Neither of us dare go out in this because we may be killed." As soon as the all-clear was sounded at 6.30am they came round to see what had happened. When they got to the junction of Hengaston Street and Avonleigh Road their way was blocked by a crater on the crossroads about thirty feet across and thirty feet deep.

There were many Civil Defence people at the site, and looking at our part of the street all they could see were great piles of debris. One of the volunteers asked what they were doing and they said they had relatives buried under the debris. The man told them that he was very sorry but if they had anyone under that they were either dead or badly injured, and that in any case they couldn't start digging until light so they may as well go home. The man left but Ada was hysterical and at that point a young sailor came along and asked her what was wrong. When she and Ewart explained he offered to climb over the debris and see if he could hear anything.

Miraculously he was able to locate where our house had been and he shone a torch into the debris, and through the gap we saw a chink of light. We all started shouting and he asked how many there were there, and then he asked if anyone was injured or dead. Then when we shouted back and he knew we were all OK he assured us that the Civil Defence would come and rescue us and in the meantime to remain calm and patient. At about 8.30am the rescuers turned up and dug until 10.30am.

The first thing to come through the tiny hole was a torch, then that was followed by a jug of tea. We were given a bit of time to drink the tea, which I think was the best and most welcome tea I've ever tasted. Then the hole was made large enough for Colin, who was six months old, to be pulled through and then the hole was further enlarged and one by one we were pulled out. We had to be carried because we all left our shoes outside the cupboard, but there were two surprises as we were carried out; the first being that a large crowd had gathered to watch the rescue and a huge cheer went up when they saw us all alive. Our second surprise was the extent of the damage, as a large part of our street was totally destroyed and what remained was badly damaged.

We were taken round the corner to Auntie Vera's and there was an emotional scene when we all met, although I was more interested in looking in the mirror as I looked as if I had been up a chimney. Aunt Vera's house was also in a terrible state; all the roof tiles had been blown off, most of the bedroom ceilings were down, the back of the house had moved away from the front, there was a large crack that you could see daylight through and every window was broken.

The electricity, water and gas supplies were also off. Her house was not the only one damaged; most of them in Hengaston Street were in a similar state, but the organisation of the Civil Defence and council people was amazing. By the end of the day water carts were visiting the streets with fresh drinking water and builders appeared from nowhere to nail temporary coverings to the smashed windows and put large tarpaulins over the roofs to keep the houses dry.

In the meantime, transport arrived to take those of us who had been bombed to a refugee centre where we were given a hot meal and a bath, then any clothing that was dirty beyond reason was disposed of and we went through to a hall where tables were laid out with clothes of all kinds for everybody that needed them including shoes, socks and slippers. It must have been a great comfort to the adults to know that we were all being taken care of with such kindness.

Three

Nailsea

We then returned to Aunt Vera's and Uncle Harry, Auntie Kate's husband, turned up. I remarked earlier that he was a bit of a wise boy and a fixer, and somehow he had managed to get hold of a post office van and Auntie Kate, Betty and Colin were whisked off to Nailsea in it. We learned later that this van belonged to a Mr Fisher, the Nailsea village postman, so they were taken to his home and stayed there until proper accommodation was found for them.

For the next ten days we all slept in the ground floor rooms at Auntie Vera's, then we had a message from Uncle Harry informing us that that Mr Fisher had heard from a family in Nailsea that they were willing to take us in. So Mother, Norman and I got on a Nailsea bus and set off for what was to be a totally new way of life. I remember that when we got off the bus, our only possessions were in a baby buggy. (What a state to be reduced to.) Eventually we found Mr Fisher's house and were reunited with Auntie Kate and her family.

Mr Fisher then put us in the van and took us on a long journey to the place where we were going to live. It was a family of three living in a two-bedroom cottage and their names were Ern and Mary Parslow and their ten-year-old daughter Glenda. It was a real shock to go into their home because the conditions we had tolerated since our bombing were their normal way of life. The cottage had no electricity, gas or mains water and, we soon learned, no flushing lavatory. The downstairs ceilings were so low that I could reach up and touch them. There was an old-fashioned fireplace with ovens on one side, but the house was incredibly warm and they were lovely people. Even as strangers we were made so welcome. On a trivet in front of the fire was a large pot full of stew, some of which was our first meal at Nailsea.

Next Mary took out hot bricks from the oven and wrapped them in woollens. We were then shown our bedroom and the hot bricks were placed in the bed to make them warm. I will never forget our first night there: the beds were spotlessly clean and everything was so quiet and peaceful, especially after what we had endured in Bristol. We couldn't have a bath because all the water had to be fetched from a nearby well, but we soon found out that Nailsea church rectory had been taken over for London evacuees and we could get a hot bath there once a week.

The lavatory at the cottage consisted of a bench with a hole in the middle, underneath which was a bucket. When it became full it had to be emptied into a hole in the garden, and this was a chore everyone had to take their turn at. In the kitchen there was a huge earthenware pan, which contained all our drinking water after it was collected from the local well. There was also an assortment of Primus and paraffin cookers, and a meat safe.

Daily life involved many tasks which were new to us, for example the oil lamps had to be topped up with paraffin and have their wicks trimmed and glasses cleaned every day. Water had to be fetched twice a day because it was a percolating well, not fed by a spring. Everyone watched each other. To make sure no one had more than their fair share of water, there was also a huge water barrel to store all the rainwater from the roof, which we used for washing our faces and clothes.

There was no refuse collection so all burnable waste was used as fuel and tins were buried in the garden to rust away. These were all part of life at Nailsea, which we had not even given a thought to in Bristol.

Nearby was a pub called The New Inn, now renamed The Blue Flame, and a general store and post office, which sold just about everything. It was run by a lady called Hilda Baker, and the neighbours met there daily for a good gossip. She provided wooden orange boxes with cushions on top for her customers to sit on and even offered them cups of tea while they chatted.

We were very near a large farmhouse called Rose Farm, where Uncle Harry had found a flat for Auntie Kate and her children. The family who lived there were called Brean and there must have been nine or ten children who all slept on the floor next to Kate's three rooms. Mr and Mrs Brean and her mother slept in a large room downstairs and at the back of the house was a room they called the dairy; the floor was paved with flagstones and there was a well with a pump in the middle.

Their lavatory was worse than ours because there was no bucket and everything dropped down into a pit. Occasionally someone had to open a hatch at the back and dig out all the waste matter. The stink was awful and in the summer it was full of flies. One other thing: the bench that you sat on had two holes and there was no bolt on the door, so quite often you sat there next to each other while doing your business!

Although Grandmother stayed with Kate she didn't sleep there; she had a bedroom in a nearby bungalow, which had mains water and a flush toilet. In many ways my grandmother was not a particularly nice person and she always said that Nailsea was the last place God ever made and He didn't finish it.

She was particularly scathing about the Brean family, whom she referred to as "cattle". Mrs Brean, who was in the late stages of pregnancy, was working in the garden one evening when her labour began. Her mother covered the bed in brown paper, got her daughter on to the bed and delivered the baby without a midwife, and to Grandmother's horror, gathered the paper and buried it in the garden. The whole thing was over in less than an hour and the following day Mrs Brean was up as usual, going about her daily chores! Even my mother was shocked, but Grandmother had a field day telling this story to her cronies in the off-licence at The New Inn.

Quite soon it was time for Norman and me to be taken to our new schools, which were about three miles from where we lived. At that time neither Mum, Norman or I had a bike, so we had to walk along the country lanes. I was completely amazed when I saw my school. It was right next to the Holy Trinity Church and I discovered there were three classes with boys and girls in each class, with a total of about ninety children attending. There were three teachers: a Mr Gunning from Hewish village near Weston taught the youngest, a Mr Gower was headmaster and his wife also taught there.

I loved the school from the day I started; it was housed in what had been a parish tithe barn. It consisted of three classes and one for infants. There were two other classes, one of which was a woodwork room but because of the wood shortage during the war that room was not used except for the daily service, when folding glass screens which separated the other two classes were folded back, making the three classes into one assembly room. There was another class which was in the annex built in the twentieth century and separated from the other classes by the boys' cloakroom. The heating was supplied by large coke stoves, on the top of which many of us placed potatoes to bake for our lunch. In those days there were no school dinners so we took sandwiches or ate baked potatoes in the classrooms.

Very soon after I started my schooling there, Mr Gower discovered I was quite good at drawing; he took the art classes and encouraged me a great deal. In fact he entered me in a competition for children all over Somerset and the subject we had to draw was an air raid. I won first prize, which was £5, and it was presented to me by the local MP at a ceremony on the village green. I am not sure to this day whether I gained the prize through artistic talent or (more probably) because I was the only competitor in Somerset who had actually experienced an air raid. I did not therefore have to rely on my imagination, but vividly remembered my own experience in Bristol. From then on Mr Gower insisted I had a great future as an artist and I was given a free hand to draw whatever took my fancy, and regular exhibitions of my work took place at the school and the takings at the door were donated to the war effort. My name was also put forward for a scholarship at the Royal West of England Academy of Art, but sadly I failed to gain an entry.

Mr Gower was also the church organist at Holy Trinity Church. This was a lovely building that was over six hundred years old and still possessed a cello, which had been used to accompany hymns before the organ was installed. He was also a keen gardener so we had a very well-kept school garden where I learned so much about gardening that fired my own enthusiasm and knowledge for the rest of my life. His wife taught literature and English, and she also was a very good teacher and introduced us to many of the classics of prose and verse. They were very different characters; he was full of fun and she on the other hand was a strict disciplinarian and I think we all stood in awe of her.

During the time I was in her class a boy gave me a baby jackdaw, which he'd stolen from a nest. Mother and I dug up worms and chopped them up and continually stuffed them into its ever-open beak. It thrived and I'm sure it regarded us as family. It lived in an elm tree in our garden and as soon as it spotted us, it would fly down and perch on us and it was always my companion when I was in the garden. I used to take it for rides on my bike and I'm sure it thought that if it perched on the handlebars, by furiously flapping its wings it was causing the bike to travel faster. It also flew in through the bedroom window and woke me up most days.

Anyway, it discovered which class I was in and sat on the windowsill outside, tapping the glass. Mrs Gower demanded to know whose bird it was and when I owned up she simply said, "Remove it!" I knew what would happen, however no one would ever dare argue with Mrs Gower so I went out and moved the bird. I was only back in the class a few minutes when it returned and resumed its tapping. I managed to persuade Mrs Gower that it only wanted to be with me and promised that if she allowed it into the classroom it would be no trouble. She relented and I brought Jack in and sure enough it sat quietly on my desk and was no trouble whatsoever. I think it was probably the only time a jackdaw attended school.

The school was unusual in that it was funded entirely by parish charities, so it was an Anglican school in the true sense of the word. Religious education was very important and we were all made to learn the Catechism from the Book of Common Prayer. The church rector, Mr Davey, a dear old gentleman in his eighty-second year, paid us regular visits in school and when he entered the class we were all expected to stand up, touch our forelocks and say, "Good day, Rector."

Another school tradition was that on Ascension Day the whole school attended the church for a service, at the end of which we were given the rest of the day off. For me the whole experience of attending Nailsea Parochial School was a happy one and I am sure that despite it being small and the classes being held in the six hundred-year-old tythe barn, I enjoyed a first-class education which has stood me in good stead all my life.

The junior school, which Norman attended, had close associations with Christ Church. The head teacher at this school was the organist and the choir mistress at this church soon discovered that Norman liked singing and got him to join the church choir. It was not long before Miss Morris persuaded me to join the choir as well. It was a good choir made up of about twenty boys, some Nailsea boys and some Bristol evacuees, and some were London evacuees.

On Sundays the regular services were Holy Communion at 8am, matins at 11am and evensong at 6.30pm. The church did not have blackout curtains for the windows so during the winter months evensong was sung at 3.30pm. The vicar, the Reverend Powell, was very keen to make sure that the standards were high and so he always attended the choir practice on Fridays to make sure the choir maintained his exacting standards.

Looking back, I enjoyed the services, especially the music, and learned a lot through being a member of that choir. Another thing I liked was that before each service Miss Morris gave a short recital of light classical music on the organ. I used to be retreat to the western gallery to sit there and listen. I suppose it was my first introduction to classical music and my father, when he was off duty and came for the weekend at Nailsea, would sit with me in the gallery and also listen, and he always said that Miss Morris was a fine organist.

I had been prepared for confirmation during the autumn of 1940 but when I was ready the blitz on Bristol began and one by one all the churches where the bishop would have confirmed me were bombed. So when we started to attend Christ Church my mother told the Reverend Powell about my situation and he arranged for me to be confirmed on March 21st 1941 at St John's Church, Clevedon. Mother and I cycled there from Nailsea and one of the hymns sung was 'Come Down, O Love Divine', which ever since that day has been my favourite hymn. Although Mr and Mrs Parslow were chapel people, on our return to Nailsea, they had prepared a wonderful confirmation tea for me.

A nativity play was performed at Miss Morris' school and I painted the scenes and took part in it. I also remember a choir outing when we went to Bristol and saw a film, *Dangerous Moonlight*, at the New Palace in Baldwin Street. The theme music for the film was the 'Warsaw Concerto', which I loved and became the first record I bought when I started work.

Another of my lasting memories of Christ Church, Nailsea was the harvest festival. The church was decorated with fruit, flowers, vegetables and farm produce and looked absolutely beautiful. In the summer of 1941, when so many ships which were bringing food and essentials from America were torpedoed and sank in the Atlantic, the country was in a critical state and there were national days of prayer when the churches were packed. I'm sure God answered our prayers because the summer that year was perfect for growing things and all the farms produced bumper harvests. Believe me, you really know what harvest thanksgiving is about when you've worked on a farm and seen the results of your work.

*

We settled in very well to our lives with the Parslow family and were very happy there. A large part of Station Road, Nailsea was occupied by fairly well-off people who employed housekeepers and gardeners. Mother worked for one of these families, so every morning all three of us set out on our bikes together, with us boys going to school and Mother going to work. Believe it or not, all three of us purchased second-hand bikes for about 50p each, which was the going rate in those days. I suppose if you took into consideration that the average wage was £2.50 per week, those bikes were not that cheap.

Mrs Parslow was a hard worker and I remember we came home one day to find she had put the dining chairs in the garden and varnished them all with quick-drying varnish and decorated the living room, and it was all put back in place by the time we got home. Mr Parslow worked at Coles Stone Quarry at Backwell, but in the evening he worked on a farm and was allowed to go shooting there, so we were always well supplied with rabbits, which Mrs Parslow skinned and cooked, and she tanned the skins and fashioned them into mittens for us.

They had two pets, a dog called Punch, who always accompanied Mr Parslow to his farm work and was a proper working farm dog, and a cat, which was Glenda's pet. It was very docile and would quite happily let her dress it in dolls' clothes including bootees and a bonnet and wheel it about in a dolls' pram. One day however it took fright and leapt out of the pram, ran to the end of the garden and jumped over the wall into the orchard at the back of the pub. We children chased up the lane alongside the gardens and went into the pub orchard, hoping to find it.

Mrs Pike, the pub landlady, was sitting on a bench and she was very upset, and said in a very broad Somerset accent, "I do feel so queer, I've just seen a pixie run through." I could well visualise how she caught a glimpse of a tiny figure running through with dolls' clothes on. Anyway, it all ended well as the cat soon returned.

Another organisation called the Home Guard was a kind of part-time army made up of men who for some reason or other were exempt from military service. The local Home Guard met regularly and after their drill got together in a shed with a corrugated iron roof, which backed on to the lane. In this shed was stored a large barrel of very strong cider, which the men partook of until they were very merry. One evening their wives waited until the men were very drunk and all of us, children included, crept up and threw masses of stones over the high wall on to the corrugated roof. There was absolute pandemonium as the men really thought the Germans had invaded. They were shouting and racing around in a drunken stupor. I think we laughed for days about it.

Soon after we settled in with Mr and Mrs Parslow it was suggested that, like all the other boys that lived around, I should get a job at a farm. I started part-time work at Mr Cook's farm, which was where Mr Parslow went shooting. The wages were in decimal coinage of 12 1/2 p per week if you turned up each evening and all day Saturday, or 25p if you were on school holiday and worked there for six full days. The money was poor but I was glad I had the experience of working there, mainly because there were no tractors on that farm, i.e. everything was done with beautiful shire horses. They were used for harrowing, ploughing, haymaking and potato-digging. I was taught how to work with these horses and then expected to muck in like everyone else. The method of farming was the same as had been practised for hundreds of years. I was quite large and stocky and was expected to work alongside the men and do the same as them.

One of the first jobs they gave me was shelling beans for cattle feed. The heap of beans was massive and I sat on a stool and shelled for weeks. Another job was watering the bull. It was chained up in the cowshed and would drink buckets of water as fast as if they were just tipped up. Sometimes I cleaned the cowsheds and pigsties, which involved shovelling up all the dung and removing it in a wheelbarrow and then washing everything down with a hosepipe. There were the henhouses to be cleaned as well, so there were a great variety of things to be done.

Then as spring approached there was more work outdoors. I remember the hayfields being harrowed before the grass grew long.

This was done by a horse pulling a contraption on a large, square latticework frame with spikes on the underside. As the frame was pulled up and down the field the spikes would dig into the surface and break up the soil and then the ground could be fertilised. The downside was that the process brought up lots of small stones to the surface, which had to be removed otherwise at mowing time they would snag the mowing machine blades and break them. So for many Saturdays I was given buckets and told to clear the field of stones, so I walked up and down filling the buckets for hours on end.

Of course there was haymaking sometime in June and then the whole community would come together to gather the hay with rakes, load it on to a cart and in some corner of the field a hay *Môn* would be built, so there were some people unloading the carts with pitchforks and the more expert ones were on top of the hay receiving the hay and spreading it to make a symmetrical shape. This was not just decorative because if the hay was built properly and roofed the hay would always remain dry until it was used next winter.

I upset Mr Cook because I found another farm that would pay me 2 1/2p per hour and that was considerably more than he was paying me. So I was learning country ways, and I would not go so far as to say country folk are mean, but I think their way of life makes them canny.

In Bristol there was a final blitz on Good Friday and the farm where Uncle Fred worked in Victoria Street was bombed, and he was offered a job at the firm's branch in Weston-super-Mare. It seemed convenient for his job that they moved to Nailsea, so their furniture was put into storage and they came to live with Mr and Mrs Hobbs quite near us. My grandmother came at just about the same time to live with Auntie Kate, so the three sisters and their mother were all now living within a half mile of each other. Then ironically the air raids stopped. I enjoyed the fact that Mona, who was about my age, came to my school and from then on Mr Gower, the head teacher, always referred to us as Auntie and Uncle.

In August of 1941 Mother became pregnant and it was realised that we could not remain at Mr and Mrs Parslow's once the baby was born so we moved to a small cottage almost next door to my school. It was a four-roomed cottage and the owner, an elderly, bedridden lady, occupied one of the downstairs rooms, so part of the routine of living there was to care for her. The facilities there were very much the same as at the Parslows' home but there was quite a large garden and I was able to cultivate it using the knowledge I was gaining in the school garden.

In the meantime Auntie Vera and Uncle Fred found a flat quite near the seafront at Weston-super-Mare. This was great because I was able to pay many visits to them. One day we were on the beach and some young RAF recruits were doing drill there. I took a donkey ride and I think the saddle must have been loose because suddenly it turned upside down and I was hanging there. The donkey bolted and ran into the sea with me hanging upside down; luckily the airmen fell out and rushed into the sea, calmed the donkey down and untangled me.

Although the air raids on Bristol had stopped, there was one very severe raid targeting Weston. This took place when the tide was out so there was a shortage of water to fight the fires. Weston people had been advised that the safest place was the beach, so many went there and the German planes dived down and killed many of them. So Vera, Fred and their two girls came back to Nailsea and moved in with us.

Just previous to this on April 28th, at the height of another air raid centred on Bath, my second brother was born at Clevedon. Mother went to the hospital two weeks beforehand and stayed for two weeks after. Norman and I were packed off to Bristol for the month and stayed with Dad's sister Auntie Dora.

When the blitz on Bristol began in November 1940 the only defence were searchlights, which combed the sky and if a German plane got picked up in the beam ack-ack guns would fire at it and try to shoot it down, but this method was not very effective. However, on the night of April 28th 1942 a different system of defence was tried. The ack-ack guns were positioned at regular sites all over the city and simply fired all the time the planes were overhead in an imaginary grid pattern. The noise was truly deafening but it was effective and that night only one bomb was dropped on Bristol, so they turned their attention to Bath.

At that time no child was allowed in a maternity hospital so I did not see Mum or my brother until she came home with him. It was quite soon after his birth that our relatives from Weston moved in with us. The cottage was quite crowded, with them all occupying one bedroom and us the other, plus Mrs Isles, the owner, in one of the downstairs rooms. However, we children had a good time and took over a disused pigsty at the bottom of the garden, which we turned into a clubhouse. Mr Ridley who lived next door was the village undertaker and he made his own coffins, so he kindly gave us a lot of elm offcuts, which we used to make a door and furniture for our den. Then we made writing pad holders, wallets for ration books and spill boxes etc., and we went round the village and sold these items from door to door. Altogether we earned about £3, which was more than a man's weekly wage then, and we sent the money to Mrs Churchill's Red Cross Aid to Russia Fund. We were very proud to receive a letter from her addressed to us all in her own handwriting, thanking us for supporting this cause.

Sadly by the end of 1942 the situation in the cottage was proving too much. Auntie Kate was allocated a house in Fairfield Road Bristol, and Mum and we three boys took over her flat at Rose Farm with the Brean family. So we now had three rooms: two bedrooms and a living room in which we lived and cooked and ate. We stayed there until 1943.

Four

Back to Bristol

There was a fundamental disagreement between my parents about our present and future lives. They had been paid about £150 compensation for the loss of our house, which in those days was a considerable sum of money. On one hand my mother, Norman and I were very happy at Nailsea, but on the other hand because of the nature of his job, including shift work, my father could not come and live with us there, so he remained with his sister Dora in Bristol and visited us at weekends.

It was possible at that time to purchase a small cottage in Nailsea for £50, which Mum was keen on doing, but Dad was adamant that as soon as possible we should all return to Bristol. Also, weight was added to his point of view by the fact that I was interviewed for a job at W D & H O Wills and I started there at the age of fourteen in 1943. So when the city council wrote and offered us a requisitioned house in Camden Road, Southville, Dad insisted that we came back to Bristol, which we did very reluctantly. However, there were compensations. The house was Edwardian and very roomy, and at last we had electricity, gas, water and proper drainage. There was also a small garden with a conservatory.

Even when we got there, Dad refused to buy any decent furniture and Mum had to scout around and buy second-hand furniture because Dad said he would not purchase new stuff until we moved back to Lynton Road. He foolishly thought it was possible to pick up the old threads and carry on life as if nothing had happened in the war years. Many years later, before he died he admitted to me that he had made a big mistake.

Soon after moving back to Bristol I started work at Wills' in August 1943. The day's work commenced at 7.20am and finished at 5.30pm with a twenty-minute breakfast break in the works canteen, then a one-hour lunch break at 12.30pm with a five-minute tea break during the afternoon. I have to say that the cooked breakfasts were excellent at very reasonable prices, and so were the lunches. With the war in progress and shortages caused by food rationing, the Wills' works canteen gave a wonderful opportunity to supplement our meagre diet.

However, to work in a manufacturing factory was an experience I hated from day one! If I complained someone would always tell me that I'd landed the best job in the world, with absolute security until retirement at sixty and my future assured, but I regarded it as a life sentence rather than a career. I suppose you could regard it as a bit like being an ant in a nest or a bee in a hive, with everyone involved in mindless activities to make the product and get it out to the public as quickly and cheaply as possible. This was all totally alien to my personality!

However, I was the dutiful eldest son and I tried to knuckle down to this life and make the best of it. My wages at the age of fourteen were £1 per week and ten shillings (or 50p) government supplement, so Mother took the £1 and I was left with the rest to pay for my entertainment etc., but she paid for my clothes and chose everything that I wore until I was eighteen because that was the general rule in those days. There was no such thing as teenage style; you simply wore what was bought for you.

Outside of working hours I gradually organised my leisure time to make up for this frustration. For one thing, I enrolled in the West of England College of Art and studied commercial art and lithography four nights each week. That was Monday, Tuesday, Wednesday and Friday. I always avoided Thursday because due to listening to concerts on the radio, I started to attend the Colston Hall concerts, which were always held on a Thursday evening. The difficulties presented by this activity were immense. I finished work at 5.30pm and had to get home, wash, change and grab something to eat; then rush to the hall because in those days concerts started at 6.30pm. Sadly I only managed to attend one concert at the Colston Hall because within a couple of days it caught fire and was gutted. All the concerts were transferred to the Methodist Central Hall in Old Market Street. The hall was considerably smaller than the Colston Hall and it was more difficult for me to get there, but the acoustics were perfect so that was a bonus.

On occasions at the weekend I rode my bike out into the countryside and painted or sketched scenes. There was one occasion when I was sitting on a railway embankment painting Chelvey Court and Church and a young soldier in uniform turned up and asked if he might watch me. I of course agreed and as I worked he told me he was from Christchurch in New Zealand and had been a prisoner of war. Upon his release he'd been sent to Chelvey Court to recover, but was now due to return home. He then said that he liked my painting very much and would like to buy it from me. I had taken to the man and agreed, and he paid me £5 on the spot and stayed with me until I'd finished the picture. I then handed it over and I presume he took it back to New Zealand.

Quite near our house in Camden Road there lived a lady who taught piano and I got to know that after her lessons finished she would continue to play for an hour or so. She was a brilliant musician and I used to stand outside her house listening to her playing. Her favourite piece was Chopin's 'Revolutionary Study', which I loved, and I often waited outside, hoping she might play my favourite piece. I wonder what might have happened if I'd had the nerve to knock on her door and ask if I could go in and listen.

I also cultivated our back garden in my spare time, and a neighbour whose bedroom overlooked it told me she loved sitting in the window and admiring my efforts. I suppose my whole life at that time consisted of my job, which I loathed, my family, which I loved, and my own efforts to overcome my frustration at working in what I saw as a dead-end job. When we first moved to Bristol I used to walk three or four miles to Long Ashton or Abbots Leigh churches for Sunday worship. In a weird sort of way I suppose my attendance at the village churches was my last tangible link with Nailsea, which I missed so much.

We always worked on a Saturday morning but the machines shut down early for a good weekly clean, and during this time weekly announcements were made over the tannoy system. However, on June 6th 1944 the warning bleeps went and the factory came to a standstill for a very important announcement. We were all told that an invasion of Europe had begun, with the Allied forces landing on the beaches in Normandy. The atmosphere in the factory was electric and I saw many of the women whose husbands were over in France breaking down and crying.

We all knew that although this could be the end of the war, a lot of our men would be killed. Although no religion was on the agenda at Wills', I know that on June 6th many of my workmates were offering up prayers. Later that year someone from St Hugh's Church paid us a visit and invited us to return to the church with him, which we did. It was a funny experience to go back there, bearing in mind our experiences of bombing, evacuation to Nailsea and all the other changes in our lives, to see things going on as if nothing had happened.

In May 1945 the war at last came to an end with victory for the Allies, and for some reason the announcement of victory came officially at midnight. When it happened there was bedlam. All the ships in the harbour sounded their hooters, fireworks were set off and crowds took to the streets and began celebrations that went on for weeks. Our house in Camden Road was not far from the city centre so I dressed and went out and joined a massive crowd all converging on the centre. When we got there the crowds were so dense that it seemed possible to walk on people's heads!

Everyone was singing and dancing and hugging one another. Someone had rigged up a music system on the roof of an air raid shelter and was blasting out dance music. Although this particular party broke up at daybreak, the following day was declared a holiday and the partying in the streets went on for days. Then the hangover started – although the war was over, austerity and rationing continued and in fact the shortages got worse and rationing was not finally abolished until 1956.

One of the nicer aspects of being a Wills' employee was that they paid an annual bonus to all their staff and it was paid at the beginning of the financial year in April, so I was paid my first bonus in April 1944: the princely sum of £5. I had recently, since starting work, become a cinema fan, so with my first bonus I bought a second-hand film projector, which showed 9.5mm movies but would only take small spools of about fifteen minutes' duration. I spent many happy hours showing my films to my friends and family. Most weekends I visited the cinema with mates from work or I took my mother; she liked the romantic films and her favourite film star was Greer Garson, so any film starring her was a must.

Although my father was instrumental in getting the family back to Bristol, he seemed to lead a very independent life from us; I think the years we had spent in Nailsea with him remaining in Bristol had driven a wedge between him and my mother and he would often come off duty, get changed and go off to a cinema alone. Another sad thing was that I think the awful experience Mother, Norman and I had undergone, especially the bombing, had changed her from the lovely, gentle person I had known before the war into an aggressive, strident person and Father just couldn't cope with it. She did confide in me that despite the breakdown in their marriage, she for her part would never consider separation or divorce because on one thing they both agreed: they owed it to us, their offspring, to remain together, and they did. Much of my time as the eldest son in my teens was spent as a go-between and sometimes counsellor when things got really bad between them.

Part of the problem was that Father was an introvert and it was impossible to persuade him to open up and talk about his marital problems.

I was lucky because a new priest came to St Hugh's who became a good friend to me, and became my ally in trying to reconcile Mother and Father. His name was Dick Kirkham. Prior to becoming a priest, he was an actor and came from a theatrical family. He told me that one of the West End theatres in London was built especially for his mother. He had also spent some time in the RAF. My father enjoyed a highly developed sense of humour, which greatly appealed to Dick so they shared common ground.

Father relished telling me about the day before the war when Mother had packed his lunch box for work and put in a Dutch steak tomato, which is about the size of a large grapefruit. When lunchtime came and the men produced their food this massive tomato was a talking point and someone asked my father where he had got it; quick as a flash he said that he'd grown it in the garden and fed it with 'bomateg'. The men remarked that they had never seen such a large tomato. Of course this was a purely fictitious word but he was so convincing that some of them got him to write it down and then scoured the seed shops in Bristol to try and track it down, and they even got some shopkeepers to try and order it. Dick loved the story and jokingly accused him of being a wicked man.

Dick was also an avid bike rider and we went on rides to the countryside and around Bristol, which I introduced him to. Unfortunately his boisterous behaviour got him into the bishop's black book and he told Dick that as long as he was bishop, unless Dick mended his ways, he would never be offered a living in the Bristol diocese.

Although I took after my father in having quite an introverted nature I had many good friends, including girls, in the factory and got about quite a lot with them. I respected and loved my parents to the extent that at times the groups I got around with were involved in some escapades that I refused to be part of.

At the age of sixteen I was given a mechanical test at work and passed it, so I began training to become a cigarette machine operator, which was a better job altogether than working in the warehouse. I think the worst part of the job was cleaning down, which we had to do at the end of each working day. Each machine was supplied with a pair of bellows, which we used to blow the tobacco dust off the machine. The dust was horrendous and I always arrived home stinking of tobacco dust.

Very late in my career at Wills' the use of bellows was stopped and we were all supplied with vacuum cleaners, and a different kind of machine was introduced that produced less dust. Although as employers went, Wills' was probably one of the best, all the dust that was involved caused TB in some employees and the firm ran a TB hospital on the top of the Mendip Hills where the victims were sent to be cured.

When the war had ended in 1945 a general election was called and Winston Churchill's coalition government came to an end. Although the country accepted that it owed Churchill a great debt a lot of servicemen who were returning to the civilian life determined that the post-war years of the Great War would not be repeated again, and what they wanted was full employment, better health and a more just society, and they decided that the Labour party would deliver this. So the result of the election was that the Labour party was voted in with a huge mandate to pursue a programme of the greatest reformation that the country had ever experienced.

Clement Atlee was the new Prime Minister and he formed a brilliant government that really did deliver what it had promised in its manifesto. The pits and the railways were nationalised and the NHS was formed in 1948, but sadly Atlee had been offered a poisoned chalice. For one thing, the war effort had bankrupted the country and in fact our post-war debt to the USA has only at the beginning of the twenty-first century, finally been paid off. Sir Stafford Cripps, who was the Chancellor of the Exchequer, had to introduce stronger austerity measures than we had experienced during the war.

Then in 1946, just after Christmas, the harshest winter in living memory set in and lasted until April 1947. We were all reduced to queuing up for coal and there was a desperate shortage of vegetables. I believe there were even places where the sea froze. Although the war had ended in Europe in May it continued until August, when it was finally brought to an end when the Americans dropped atomic bombs on Hiroshima and Nagasaki and the Japanese surrendered.

Two things I remember of life at Camden Road: the radio, which we had managed without during our stay in Nailsea, had three programmes we always listened to, which were *These You Have Loved*, presented by Doris Arnold, which consisted of classical music that listeners requested. Then there was *Appointment With Fear*, presented by Valentine Dyall, who had the kind of voice that frightened you to death and his stories were equally terrifying. Then there was the BBC's first sitcom, called *ITMA*, or to give it its full title, *It's That Man Again*. Tommy Handley was the main character and the programme took place in an office. It was very witty and funny and I well remember some of the characters and their catchphrases.

There was Mrs Mop, the office cleaner who spoke with a cockney accent and her catchphrase was, "Can I do you now, sir?" Then there was a drunken colonel whose slurred catchphrase was, "I don't mind if I do." Then there was a woman called Mona Lott, who always told a tale of woe and misfortune, and her catchphrase was, "It's being so cheerful that keeps me going." Then there was a villain called Phooph, who spoke with a perfect German accent and parodied a German-sympathising broadcaster called Lord Haw-Haw, who always broadcasted the day after any city had been bombed and mocked us. I'm sure *ITMA* was the inspiration for *The Goon Show*, which started a few years later and starred ex-servicemen like Harry Secombe and Spike Milligan and made them household names. Even Prince Charles asked to be a guest on one of their programmes.

Quite soon after we moved into the house one of the neighbours told my mother she was selling her house and moving. Mum got in touch with Auntie Vera and Uncle Fred at Nailsea and the result was that they bought the house and came to live next door but one to us, and remained there until they both went into a care home. Early in 1946 Mother became pregnant again; she was then about forty years old, which at that time was quite old to be pregnant. Furthermore, she was not well and cystitis set in, and then to add to the misery, the council informed us that our house in Lynton Road was being rebuilt and we were offered the chance to return there. We would have preferred to stay at Camden Road, partly because it was spacious and very near Wills' factory, and also because we were very happy in that neighbourhood, but Father was quite insistent that we moved. By this time Mother was very large and in fact when the baby was born on November 2nd at Bristol Maternity Hospital he weighed eleven pounds!

During Mother's pregnancy, due to Father's shift work I was often late for work and took a lot of time off to care for her. One feature of Wills' was that the firm, large though it was, had not become a public shareholding company and the family were still in charge. There was a member of the Wills family on management staff in each factory and they made it their business to visit all departments on a regular basis. When they entered the workroom they would be briefed by the foreman about the workers they would talk to. I was particularly impressed when the foreman brought the manager to my machine and he asked me about my situation at home. The firm was very strict about timekeeping and attendance; in fact if you were late three times in a month, even if only by one minute, you would be sent home for the day and lose your pay. With this in mind I was quite amazed when this manager told me not to worry about my timekeeping and attendance as they would understand, and if I experienced any more problems I was to contact the personnel department to see how they might help.

The Wills family were Congregational Christians and I am sure this influenced the way they ran their business. In the early days when the firm first opened in Bristol they owned a large house in Somerset Street in Kingsdown, and every Sunday one of their employees was invited to lunch with the family. When we moved back into Lynton Road we must have moved in too soon after the builders because the house was cold and damp, with condensation on most of the walls. Just after Christmas in 1946 the coldest winter in UK history began, and the freeze lasted until April. I was eighteen years old in February so I was conscripted for national service. Then a letter came in January stating that due to the severe winter all conscription was suspended until further notice because all the camps were closed.

Five

Conscription and Training

Eventually I received my call-up papers and was ordered to report for duty at Reservoir Camp, Gloucester at 10.30am on Monday May 22nd to begin six weeks' primary training. To give some idea of how late the thaw came, the intake that was leaving camp when we arrived were still shovelling snow and clearing ice six weeks before.

We were all ushered into the canteen and given large slices of fruit cake and drinking chocolate, or cocoa as it was known then. Next we were divided into platoons, each with its own sergeant and corporal, and I think the first thing the sergeant said was that he regarded us all as showers of shit but from now on he was going to make soldiers of us. We were informed that from now until we were demobbed we would not be asked to do anything, but would be ordered and would obey the orders of anyone from lance corporal upwards, and always salute them. It was also compulsory to carry your soldier's pay book wherever you went and to know your army number. I am generally no good at figures but was so frightened of the consequences that I kept a piece of paper in my top pocket with my number on it and took it out to read frequently. To this day I have remembered it; it was 19171124.

Anyway, we were marched to the two huts allocated to our

platoon. Then we went to the quartermaster's store and passed a row of tables with other soldiers standing behind them. As we passed down the room they threw items of army clothing at us, so that by the time we reached the end of the room we were completely fitted out except for boots, rifles, blankets and straw biscuit mattresses and pillows. We all struggled back to our hut and were ordered to throw everything on the floor, and the theory was that with fourteen complete sets of kit in a pile, the chances were that we would find something to fit, and strangely enough we did! Then we changed into our uniforms, and I must admit we did look a sight.

After we had collected our rifles we were set to cleaning them, and then we practised our first drill with our sergeant bullying and chivvying us. One mercy was that the first day seemed to pass in a flash. From then on it was six weeks of drill, rifle-cleaning, blancoing gaiters and belts etc., and drill. There was also shooting on the range and practice jabbing of stuffed sacks with our bayonets. Every Saturday there was a mass parade on the barrack square and if a platoon came up to scratch they were dismissed for the weekend, so it was a good incentive to try to drill properly. Those of us who lived near enough could then hitch-hike home. My family, having given me a tearful farewell on Thursday, were amazed to see me again on Saturday.

At camp we spent a lot of time outdoors for drill and on the firing range, and in lectures and generally learning the basics of becoming a soldier, and much to my surprise I enjoyed it. I was free at last of some of the worries of home life and I know all the exercise and open air made me healthier and more muscular. Another good thing was that because national service was compulsory for all young men in Britain, it brought together all kinds of people from all kinds of backgrounds, which broadened our outlook on life.

The biggest downside was the ever-present awareness that our freedom was sacrificed for as long as we were in the services. A good example of this was that one day I was stood at a bus stop in Gloucester and an officer came to the same one. Immediately I sprang to attention and saluted him until he said the magic words,

"At ease, soldier" – then I could relax. We were also told that if we were out in uniform and a funeral passed us we would remove our hats and wait until it had passed.

At some time during our primary training we were all interviewed by a personnel selection officer, whose job it was to try and match the talents and capabilities of each recruit with the requirements of the army at that particular time. I was very lucky because I appeared to hit it off with the officer who interviewed me. He was aware I had been downgraded because of flat feet and it would not be possible to send me to a regiment, so something had to be done to slot me into one of the corps.

He asked me about my pre-service life, such as work and hobbies. I explained to him that I had attended the West of England College of Art for four years doing commercial art and lithography, and that I liked classical music. This was one of his passions as well, so we spent some time discussing our likes and our preferences of particular pieces of music. I think he was prodding to see if I was genuine or pulling a fast one. Then we got on to the art studies and he said that the Royal Engineers' survey department was looking for a map artist, and with my experience I might be suitable.

So when I completed my primary training I was posted to the RE training school, which was based in an ex-USA army hospital in the grounds of Longleat House in Wiltshire, which was only thirty miles from Bristol. I was over the moon, and on the day that I was posted I sent Mum and Dad a telegram giving them the news and saying that I would have time to kill at Temple Meads station while I waited for the train to Warminster. They came and met up with me and we chatted and had a snack while we waited.

When my train arrived at Warminster, transport was waiting to take me to the camp and when I arrived I reported to the duty officer. He told me that the whole camp had shut down for annual leave and that the best thing to do was to allocate me to a hut where I was to stay, get rid of my gear there and report back to him. When I did this, to my astonishment he said that he was going to send me on leave till the rest of the camp returned, which was in about two weeks. So he gave me all the ration tickets and a railway warrant! Mum and Dad were gobsmacked when I sent them another telegram saying that I was coming home for two weeks' leave. How jammy can you get?

When I returned to camp I was met with a problem. An officer who interviewed me said that they had only taken on students in the Royal Engineering School who, previous to being in the army, had been employed by the Ordnance Survey producing maps and surveying. Nevertheless, because it was the personnel officer's mistake in posting me to Longleat, I was informed that I would sit a test to see if I was to go on the course to train as a litho draughtsman producing maps.

For this test I was given a piece of one-inch-to-the-mile map and told to make an accurate copy of it. The work was very intricate because I had to draw it using a magnifying glass. I don't quite know how I managed it but I passed the test and was accepted for training, which lasted from July to December, and I successfully passed out as a four-star qualified draughtsman. In monetary terms this meant that my pay as a sapper was equal to a corporal in the infantry.

The camp was in beautiful countryside on a hill just above Longleat House, which at that time was being used as a boarding school for girls, which was of course off limits to us.

All of us took our turn with guard duty in a hut at the camp gate. The duty entailed checking on everything entering or leaving the camp. There was a small coke stove in the hut to keep us warm during the night hours. The light and the warmth attracted the deer for which Longleat is still famous, but you got used to it but it could be quite unnerving to see pairs of eyes looking at you in the darkness and gradually moving towards you. Usually, because you were sitting quite still in the hut, the deer would come right up to the hut and tap on the window with their antlers.

One daft thing happened at Longleat which I am sure could only happen in the services. We were encouraged to do sport and someone suggested that a level area could be turned into a football pitch. We imagined that a mowing machine would be provided to cut the grass but in true military style, on one Wednesday afternoon, all the personnel available in camp were marched to the proposed football field and issued with pairs of scissors to cut the grass. The stupidity of all this was that all those pairs of scissors probably cost more than a mower.

I also remember a notice going up asking for musical soldiers to report to a duty sergeant. Someone warned me way back to never volunteer for anything, so despite my love of classical music I didn't volunteer. When the men reported for duty six people were selected, and what they were made to do was shift a piano from one end of camp to the officers' mess at the other end.

I made friends with a lad from London while at Longleat. He lived in Gray's Inn Road with his widowed mother. Bert Jones was his name, and he was a typical cockney. The camp usually closed at the weekend and if we were able we went home if we lived near enough; some weekends you could get a thirty-six-hour pass and sometimes a forty-eight-hour pass. As it was not practical for thirty-six-hour passes for Bert to go to London he often came to Bristol with me and stayed with my family. It was very funny because he had never visited the West Country and I am sure he thought Bristol was a kind of village and that, when at home, we Bristolians wore farming smocks, sucked pieces of straw and drank cider. When he came to Bristol he was quite amazed that we even had a bus service, but I was able to show him so much he came to love Bristol.

In return for my hospitality he took me to London sometimes on the forty-eight-hour pass. I shall never forget my first visit because on the Thursday Bert realised that he needed a haircut and it was too late to visit a barber, so he tried to persuade me to cut it for him. I've never cut anyone's hair and in any case we didn't have any sharp scissors. He persuaded me to use a razor and shaving soap. His hair was very fine so it came away easily, but the effect was a disaster. Below his hat line he appeared to be bald, but he didn't care because he knew he would pass the gate inspection as he left.

However, when we got to London and his mother saw him she thought he'd gone bald, and with a strong cockney accent she said, "Gawd, Bert, what have they done to ya?"

I loved going to London with Bert because I got to see so many famous sites for the first time, and the great city was particularly welcoming for those of us doing national service. There was a Nuffield Centre, where if you called in and you were wearing uniform there was always a selection of tickets being handed out free, giving admission to many of the West End shows. It was also my first trip on the Tube, which I found fascinating.

The Longleat camp was very beautiful because it was set in the middle of woodland and parkland and the autumn was very lovely when the bracken turned gold and the leaves changed colour. The food was pretty awful though. Sadly we couldn't do anything about it because when an orderly officer visited us when we were eating and asked us if there were any complaints, he was always accompanied by one of the head camp cooks. If anyone dared to complain their name was taken, and it was woe betide them next time they did the cookhouse fatigues. So we all kept our mouths shut but I knew, from when it was my turn to do cookhouse fatigues, that first-class food was delivered to the camp but it was being ruined by bad cooking.

A large concrete and breeze block hut in the camp had been adapted to make a cinema/theatre and next to it was an identical hut that served as a games room with skittles, darts and billiards, for the use of which you had to pay an attendant. This person was someone who was on fatigues. One night I was doing this duty and at the end of the evening my duty was to lock up the games room and take the cash to a Corporal 'Sleepy' Curtis, who was a regular soldier and the projectionist at the cinema.

The projection room was in a gallery at the back of the cinema, approached only by a ladder going up through a trap door. When I took the money to the cinema a film was still showing and I was faced with a problem as to how I could hand the money over. So as silently as possible, I crept up the ladder, opened the trap door and touched Corporal Curtis on his leg. I think I scared him to death.

He yelled and in the commotion broke the film, swore loudly at me and then pandemonium broke out in the cinema. I threw the money bag and games room keys into the projection room, and by then Curtis had put the cinema lights on and everyone could see me sheepishly coming down the ladder to make a hasty exit. I think the audience found it more entertaining than the film.

The company also had a drama club and sometimes plays were performed in the cinema, and there was an annual pantomime which was quite spectacular. There were two performances, a clean version for the officers and their families and a dirty version for the rest of us, which was probably one of the funniest and bawdiest shows I've ever seen. It was called *Clinkernella*. There was a scene for three ballet dancers, all three being males. They were dressed in tutus and looked every bit the part. They had Russian-sounding names corresponding with the three processes of map-making. There are the topographers who go out with the theodolites and actually survey from trig points, which are triangular concrete posts set at fixed position in a triangular pattern all over the UK. Then there are litho draughtsmen, who draw all this information on paper to create the maps. So the dancers were called Topovski (the surveyors), Trigonowski (the concrete posts) and Lithonia (the litho draughtsmen like me).

Bawdiness is something we British love, hence the popularity of the seaside comic postcards, which used cartoon drawings and double entendres bordering almost on pornography with a funny twist. A comedian from the '60s named Dick Emery, who was often on TV, was very good at this. As part of his act he dressed up as a tarty woman, who always seemed to bump into a man in the street, who would make a suggestive remark to 'her' with a double meaning. 'She' would always look shocked, then slightly amused, and then say the catchphrase that we all waited for – "Ooh, you are awful…but I like you." Then she would give the man a poke in the chest, which sent him flying. There was a lot of talent in Longleat camp and it really came into its own in the annual pantomime.

The training course finished just before Christmas 1947 and the whole camp closed down. Everyone went on Christmas leave except some unfortunates, of whom I was one, who stayed to do Christmas guard. This was a bind but on Christmas Day officers came to our billets and brought us a cup of tea and served Christmas lunch to us, and for once the food was really good.

When the rest of the camp returned those of us who had done Christmas guard were sent on leave. I was told that I would be posted to the Far East and was therefore given one whole month's leave, then almost on the last day I was sent a telegram ordering me to report to Barton Stacey camp where I would prepare for a posting to Germany. Had the authorities known this in the first place I would only have had a week's leave, so I was really lucky.

Six

Germany

I met Bert at Liverpool Street station and his mother saw us off on the train to Harwich, and then we boarded a troopship and sailed overnight to the Hook of Holland. I was quite excited because it was the first ever time that I'd been overseas. The train we caught from the Hook took us through Holland and we crossed the border into Germany at a place called Bentheim and finally arrived at Osnabrück where we stayed overnight in a disused German army barracks. I was very impressed with the facilities; there were decent toilets, showers and multi-storey accommodation blocks, all to a very high standard.

The following morning we were assembled, then divided into groups according to the various postings to which we were assigned. My destination was Bad Oeynhausen; I caught the train and when I arrived there were two soldiers from my billet to meet me at the station. My first impression of the town was very positive; it was completely undamaged in the war and I was told that in pre-war days it was a holiday resort and a spa town, but it was now HQ for the British Army of the Rhine. Of course arriving in Germany in January was bitterly cold, and it snowed a lot.

The billet where I was to stay was in the main street opposite the station and was called Klosterstraße, and my quarters were on the upper floors of a building that was once a *bierstube*, a bar. I was introduced to the rest of the staff in the building and then shown to my room. I found it very hard to believe that I was to have a room to myself, and the final surprise was that I was taken up into the attic and invited to pick whatever furniture I needed from the collection there, and it was all good quality civilian furniture, not army issue. Then I was taken to an army store where I collected bed sheets, blankets, cutlery and crockery.

By then it was lunchtime and I was taken to the cookhouse, which was amazing. Although it was housed in a large Nissen hut all the tables had tablecloths and German waitresses served us at our tables, and the food was superb. It was explained to me that all this luxury with the food was to drive home to the Germans that we had won the war and were there as an army of occupation. By comparison with the general population, the Germans who worked for us were well paid and also well looked after, so they were very eager to please.

After lunch I was shown to my own office, which was a fully equipped drawing office. It was like a dream come true and I could not believe my luck. I found out that the whole town had been requisitioned as BAOR HQ and all the civilian population moved out. The main hotel was a vast building called the Königshof and had been requisitioned as the HQ building. The only guard duty we did was in guarding the entrance and patrolling the corridor at night.

Dotted around the town were a number of clubs run by charities to entertain us. There was a TOC H, a Wesley House, a Salvation Army and set in beautiful parklands was a massive baroque building that had once been the main spa building. This was now the NAAFI. We sometimes went there in the evening for a cheap supper and to listen to a small German orchestra. There were also two very good town cinemas so most of us went out and socialised somewhere each evening.

I joined the garrison church and sang in the choir, and it was there I met David Barnes; we were good mates until we were demobbed and I still keep in touch with him. A small group of us took on the responsibility to see that evening prayer was said daily in the church. It was a great joy to belong to the church because for one thing the chaplain explained to me that when we entered the doors, we left rank behind us. A good example of this was that each Sunday one or other of the officers who lived in the married quarters would invite us to Sunday lunch with their family. I was particularly grateful to Captain Ken Newing who, incidentally, many years after his demob, became a priest and finally an Anglican bishop.

I never smoked or drank so I always had plenty of cash and I chose to send part of my army pay home to my parents. An advantage of this was that if something terrible happened to me I was advised that my family would be eligible to a lot of compensation. Anyway, each week we would indent for the amount that we required and I always applied for less than my entitlement. One week I put in for my usual amount but it was refused; the reason I was given was that my account was overdrawn. I knew enough about army regulations to know that I could not query this with the captain, who was the garrison paymaster.

I brought this up with Ken and he told me that every soldier is entitled to ask for his pay book to be scrutinised at his regimental headquarters in Britain, so I should take my book to the paymasters office and demand this and they wouldn't dare refuse me. In the meantime, he said that because he knew I was telling the truth he would lend me whatever I needed till it was sorted out. I took Ken's advice and thanked him for his offer and I took my pay book to my billet sergeant and asked for it to be scrutinised at the Royal Engineers Regiment HQ UK. My book was sent off and scrutinised and when it came back it was with an apology and the good news that I was hugely in credit and the restrictions must end immediately.

I learned later that the particular officer who had been involved in this affair was under investigation by the army police. He was eventually court-martialled and found guilty of doing this with many soldiers' pay, as he had done with mine. My name was not mentioned and thankfully I didn't suffer the embarrassment of appearing in court, but what had happened to that officer was the talk of the garrison and I was deeply thankful for my membership of the garrison church and my friendship with Ken.

Trips were often organised for us to travel to Hanover to attend an opera or a concert, and on one occasion transport was laid on for us to attend the first music festival to be held in Germany after the war. It was at Bad Pyrmont and featured the Berlin Opera and Philharmonic Orchestra. I remember seeing *The Marriage of Figaro* and *Così Fan Tutti*, both by Mozart. David Barnes and I attended as many events like this as was possible as it was the chance of a lifetime for music lovers.

All the different skilled corps of the army had their directorates where I was stationed at HQ BAOR, so I was in RE survey directorate and all the army top brass were also based there. So was the control commission; that was the equivalent of the Civil Service. Then of course there was the garrison which organised military things including the Redcaps or Royal Military Police. They controlled the streets and you could be pulled in if you were not properly dressed, or if you were caught breaking the night curfew.

On one occasion they pulled me over and wanted to know why I was wearing brown leather gloves. I tactfully pointed out that they were my own gloves. They replied that only commissioned officers were allowed to wear leather gloves and that in future I was to wear the ordinary army issue of khaki woollen gloves. We were also made to wear either black shoes or boots, not brown. Because I was flat-footed I was allowed to wear shoes, but for anyone wearing boots the MPs could order them to lift their feet and the boot soles were checked to make sure the regulation number of steel studs were in place.

The British zone in Germany had its own radio station called the British Forces Network, and once a week they linked up with the BBC and ran a programme called *British Forces Favourites*. I think the anchorman in Germany was Cliff Michelmore and the one in London was Jean Metcalfe. On one occasion I had the

Warsaw Concerto played for my family and Cliff sent them a message. As you can imagine the programme was very popular with the troops in Germany and their families in the UK.

If there was any downside it was that I did not meet many Germans, except those who worked for us, due to the fact that Bad Oeynhausen was a garrison town full of British personnel. One nice thing was that Bert Jones, the Londoner with whom I was friendly at the Longleat camp and who had been posted to Minden, when we arrived in Germany was seconded to our town to work in a letterpress factory and was given quarters in my billet.

Looking back I think that my time in Germany was the best time of my life up to that point. I had good friends, a really interesting job, a better room than I had ever had in my life and a very happy church life. It was also a luxury to love my family at a distance without complications. As for home leave, well, I enjoyed frequent visits to the UK. The biggest and longest challenge I faced in Germany was due to the commencement of the Cold War by the Russians. Soon after I was posted they blockaded Berlin and I think we feared that we were in for another war with yours truly in the front line. The Berlin airlift began with Dakota aircraft flying in to the Berliners in the British zone of the city, carrying vital food supplies and other necessities. They were landing at Tempelhof Airport every few minutes.

The Russians also attempted another tactic. When the war ended and Germany was divided into British, American, French and Russian zones, no one, except maybe Churchill, anticipated future trouble so the boundaries between the zones were very perfunctory, sometimes a small stream or even a garden fence. When the Cold War began the Russians disputed the boundaries and sometimes kidnapped anyone who strayed into what they alleged was their territory. This happened so often that the military were afraid of an incident so severe that it could ignite a real conflict.

I was ordered to report to the military equivalent of MI5 in the Königshof and filled in on the gravity of the situation, but sworn to secrecy. Their solution was that I as HQ draughtsman would work with them and produce a complete set of diplomatic maps showing all the disputed areas. Once I started I had to report to their office each day and they would give me all the information I needed to work with for the following day. The work was so sensitive I had to work on my own with the office door locked; then at the end of the day I would take the work back to their office. I continued to do this until I had completed all the maps, which covered all the British and Russian zones where they met. I would also guess that the French and the Americans had to do the same, and although I was not thanked I had the satisfaction of knowing later that it worked because there was no more kidnapping. Did I save the world from World War III? We shall never know but I rate this as the most important job I did in Germany.

There were two very special events in the garrison church, which I shall always remember. On Easter Sunday in 1948 the morning service was broadcast and relayed by the BBC in the UK, and my family listened to it and I felt very close to them during that service. Then later in the year the Archbishop of York paid us a visit and David Barnes and I were his servers at Holy Communion. He was very elderly and I think his name was Dr Garbett. We all felt very honoured that he had visited us.

One of our friends at the garrison church was a regular soldier about forty years old; his name was Willie Allen and he came from Norwich. He was quite a character; very high church and always singing hymns to the Virgin Mary, and he loved his pint of beer. He radiated joy and was certainly not pious. Once I was demobbed I lost track of him except when I met him at David Barnes' wedding, for which I travelled to David's home at Great Chart near Ashford in Kent.

Sadly Willie gave rise to a part of my life I bitterly regret, and for which I've always been ashamed. After David's wedding I didn't hear from Willie until I received a letter from him asking if he could come to Bristol and stay with me, as he had a friend there that he had cause to visit. I don't usually stand on my dignity but on this occasion I thought I was not prepared for him to make use of me, so I ignored his letter. Sometime later David got in touch with me and told me that Willie had committed suicide by drowning in a canal in Norwich. The question that haunted me and has done all my life is, was that letter from Willie really a cry for help, and had I responded, might it have prevented him from committing suicide? I shall never know but to this day I wish I had answered his letter.

During the whole of my army career I was ribbed about my Bristol accent, which I admit to having and am quite proud of it, but I know it is quite mild as accents go. I rarely had the chance to prove this during my army career except when I brought Bert Jones to Bristol, took him about the city and he heard some truly strong accents and could not understand a word that was said. We were sitting in the NAAFI one evening when someone I'd worked with at Wills' spotted me. We didn't expect to meet because neither of us knew that the other was there. Anyway, he bore down on us and we had a nice chat but this person, Bert Miles, had a really strong Bristolian accent and after he had left, David and the other mates I was with asked me what language we were talking in!

I had proved my point and triumphantly, I simply stated, "That was a true Bristol accent", and at last the ribbing stopped.

The unique character of the Bristol accent is that the way we use grammar is unique and in some way medieval. A small example would be that if someone with a broad accent wanted to know how someone else was, they wouldn't say, "How are you?" Even in broad Bristolese the question would be phrased, "Ow bist thee?" Well, 'thee' and 'thou' are medieval versions of 'you', and 'bist' is almost 'be ist', which is a medieval version of 'are'! Bristolians always put the letter L on the end of words where it should not be. For example, 'a malaria area' in the Bristol accent would be 'a malarial areal' and also a seal (as in the sea creature) is pronounced 'sill', and paradoxically a windowsill is pronounced 'window seal'. Another word which is almost always pronounced wrong is 'certificate', which becomes 'cerstificate'.

I once attended French lessons at night school and the teacher, who was not a Bristolian, said that our accent is very unusual in that not only was there a true Bristol accent but within it there were sub-accents depending on the part of Bristol you lived in. To prove this point he promised us that he did not have any written proof of what part of Bristol we were from, but as an exercise he got each of us to say something individually and from that he guessed where we lived, and he was accurate to within a couple of streets. It was quite amazing.

I shall write later in this autobiography of the time when for two years I worked as a chaplain at the BRI. I was doing rounds in one of the wards and one of the patients shouted out, "Yer, I knows you." That is a good Bristol accent for, "Here, I know you."

Maybe I should have mentioned earlier that David Barnes was a gifted organist and a pianist, and that part of my enjoyment of him was listening to him play. In fact in the Wesley House club there was a piano in the chapel, which the authorities kept in tip-top condition for him to play. Another nice feature of Bad Oeynhausen was that there were spa bathhouses with lots of cubicles in which there were large oak baths, and attendants were on hand to fill them with hot spa water for us to take a bath in.

In front of the Kurhaus Theatre there was a large fountain which pumped spa water to a height of about eighty feet, just like the one at Chatsworth House in Derbyshire. The garden surrounding the spa bathhouses and Kurhaus were also kept in immaculate condition by an army of gardeners. In the same park stood the Kurhaus Theatre, a beautiful baroque-style theatre in which there were regular plays and concerts. The whole experience of being at Bad Oeynhausen was like holidaying at a tip-top resort with all the facilities free.

I visited Hamlin, the town of the legend of the pied piper. It was a pretty town full of old timber-fronted houses and we saw the cave where the piper took the children of the town and sealed them up forever. The damage to Hanover was terrible; in fact I did not see much of the town because it was flattened and its citizens were living under the piles of debris in what must have been the cellars of the buildings. The people we saw looked as if they were starving, a far cry from the legend of Hitler's master race!

Another important thing happened during my time in Germany was the conversion of the Reichsmark into the Deutschmark. I do not know anything about the American, French or Russian zones but from my experience in the British zone it was truly a black market economy. You could purchase anything by using cigarettes, coffee, chocolate or even soap as a currency. Generally speaking traders preferred this rather than proper currency.

We had a German girl who came and cleaned our quarters and she would also take our laundry home, but she told me not to pay her in currency but to give her extra soap as she could trade this for food. With the economy in this state it was really not worth working for a wage and I think the authorities were alarmed that there could be hyperinflation leading to future problems with Germany. So what happened was that an announcement was made that on a certain date the banks would exchange a limited amount of the old Reichsmarks for an equivalent in the new Deutschmarks, and beyond the monetary ration all currency was worthless. The strategy really worked. Overnight thousands of black marketeers went broke and within weeks shops were accepting the new Deutschmark. So for example you could no longer go into a shop and purchase a camera for a couple of packets of cigarettes, and from that date the German economy really took off and prospered. It has to be said however that such drastic action could only be taken in a country where its defeat in war had caused it to be under the jurisdiction of another power.

One last opportunity was offered to me before demob. The assistant chaplain sent for me and told me that I had impressed the staff of that department to the extent that they were prepared to offer me a job in their department of the control commission. This commission is the equivalent of the Civil Service. The pros were that it would give me a good future career and I would retire with a good pension. The cons were that I could be sent anywhere in the world where there was a British Army presence, and that included Korea, where at that time war was raging. So on balance I turned this opportunity down, which I have regretted ever since. This was probably one of my biggest ever mistakes.

Seven

Demob and Resettling

I went out to Germany in January 1948 and was there until May 1949. Then I returned to the UK for debriefing at Aldershot prior to my final journey home. One final tiny niggle was that at Aldershot all my military gear and clothes were handed back except what I was wearing, and I was given a large bag into which I was to pack my uniform and shirt and post it back to the authorities, and only then would they pay me my demob pay.

I can well remember the thoughts that passed through my mind as I sat alone waiting for my final train journey home to Bristol. For one thing I was alone and that was quite strange after two years of being in the company of other men all the time. For another thing, at last I was free and there would be no more orders to obey. There was also a feeling of anticlimax and wonder about the future. Being conscripted into the army was a bit like serving time in an open prison without having committed a crime.

When I arrived back home everyone was naturally very glad to see me but Mother was not at all pleased when I told her I was going to use my month's demob leave to try and find another job. The old mantra was trotted out: "You've got a first-class job with Wills' so get back there and do not complain." She could not be blamed for her attitude because there was no way she could understand my army experience.

However, day after day I contacted different firms and even produced good army references but it was all to no avail. Then something Bert Jones (who before his time in the army had been apprenticed to the print industry) said came to mind. He said, "The print industry is a completely closed shop and unless you have served an apprenticeship from the age of sixteen and you are a member of the Print Union no one is going to employ you." Sadly my month of fruitless searching proved him right.

So with a very heavy heart I went back to my old job. On the day that I started I set out from home on the same old bike I had used two years before and the thought struck me that despite my experiences during my two years' national service, I was back in the same old hole that two years previously I had jumped out of; nothing had changed except me.

I resumed my civilian life in a state of resentment but I made up my mind on one thing: I would try not to let my utter disappointment get me down, or let others see it. When I went back into my old workroom many of the people there were even working in the same place on the same machines. It was as if nothing had happened except to me, and that was only some flight of fancy.

I also returned to St Hugh's Church and picked up my old friendship with Dick Kirkham. I was quite sorry for him because when I was away he developed a slipped disc and was in constant pain. It was finally put right by an operation called a spinal fusion, which at that time was something new.

Dick had a real gift for bringing people together and during his time at St Hugh's he breathed a lot of new life into the church. This was also good for me because I recommenced the boys' choir, which I had been running before my national service. We had a church organist who was a dear soul but quite mad and eccentric. Psalms are most probably the most difficult of all types of church music either to play or to sing and Grace would often make mistakes. She would shout, "Damn" in a loud voice and slam the lid of the piano down. She also, for no reason, had fits of giggles and often handed round sweets to the boys in the choir, so it could be difficult for me trying to train them and make them take things seriously and her sometimes egging them on to mess about.

Sadly things reached a crisis at a church meeting and she was asked to resign. Although on one hand I was relieved, I was also sorry for two reasons. At Grace's home she had a really fine harmonium with a double manual keyboard and a good pedal board so that with someone to pump the bellows and a competent organist, really fine tunes could be produced. She gave it to the church.

I was realistic enough to be aware that it would be difficult to attract an organist to play in a mission church on a council estate and I was proved right. Sometimes we were not certain if there would be anyone to play the following Sunday. Eventually I managed to secure the services of a girl about my age who was taking organ lessons at Christ Church, Clifton. She realised she needed somewhere to play regularly to gain experience and skills to become a proper organist. Her name was Margaret Vanes and she and I really hit it off, and, as well as playing for us at St Hugh's, she was my first girlfriend. I was fully aware that once she acquired the necessary skills she would move on to a proper appointment. It was good while it lasted but my mother did her best to sabotage the friendship; she was overly possessive towards me.

The musical highlight of Margaret's time with us was the wedding of a member of our congregation. Margaret was on holiday so she got her teacher to come from Christ Church and play for us. He was marvellous and the boys really sang like angels. It was probably the highlight of my time as choirmaster. I also started a youth club at St Hugh's, which was quite a success and built up a community of young people for the church.

1951 was the centenary of the Great Exhibition of 1851, held in the Crystal Palace in Hyde Park. Our government decided that there should be another exhibition in London because it could help to shake off the post-war drabness, and invited people from all over the world to visit us and see our achievements. 1951 was designated Festival of Britain Year and a large site on the south bank of the Thames was set aside for the main exhibition. It took a year or two to build the site. Some of the best architects and engineers were employed and the end result was spectacular. It ushered in a whole new style in design of just about everything, but at the end of the year it was all demolished except the Festival Hall, which still survives.

Everyone throughout the country was invited to do something special within their own communities, and at St Hugh's we decided to floodlight the church and tidy up the large churchyard. We organised a visit from Wills' to see the London Exhibition and I took Mum and the boys to visit *HMS Campania* which was a floating version of the London exhibition in Avonmouth docks. It was quite a year. The churchyard had always been a problem but it was largely solved after the clean-up by letting a neighbour keep a couple of goats in there, and they did a good job. Unfortunately on one Sunday it was quite windy and one of our congregation was wearing a straw hat. A gust of wind caught it, blew it over the railings and before the young lady could retrieve it a goat ate it.

The mother of the person who owned the goats had a horse and cart and was a rag and bone dealer. She could often be seen riding through Bedminster on her horse like some wild female charioteer. Anyway, she eventually became elderly and frail and one day the woman who owned the goats told me that her mother was very ill and asked me to pray for her. I told her that if her mother agreed we would visit her, which we did. Her sick room was full of anxious neighbours and when we began to pray, they all lit cigarettes. I was a bit taken aback but our vicar said afterwards that they did this to concentrate on the praying. Miraculously she recovered. She did have a recurrence of the illness and when I said that I thought her daughter should call the doctor, she flatly refused and her daughter said, "She swears by you church people."

Another great event in 1951 was the reopening of the restored Colston Hall, at that time said to be acoustically the best concert hall in Europe. Sir Thomas Beecham conducted the Royal Philharmonic

Orchestra for this concert and I still have the programme.

Quite soon after Dick Kirkham moved to another church and his replacement was a totally different kind of person. He was very pious and he even looked up at the ceiling every time he mentioned Jesus. I used to organise regular socials and dances at the church that were very popular with the parishioners and brought in a good regular income for the church. The thing was that a small group of middle-aged ladies would dress up in Union Jack knickers and do the cancan and I dreaded our new curate turning up in the middle of this spectacle. He kept saying, "I really must pay you a visit." Knowing how pious he was, I always put him off. One night, however, he turned up unexpectedly just as the ladies were doing the cancan. He was absolutely horrified and said, "Really, Desmond, I am quite appalled that you have turned our little church into a den of iniquity. This must stop." I don't think I was being helpful by sniggering and pointing out that this activity was contributing more to the church funds than the Sunday collections.

Apart from taking the Sunday services, he kept himself to himself and didn't get involved in any activities. If he was invited he always responded by saying that he really must get home to his dear wife, and incidentally, she rarely came to church.

On one occasion my father asked if he would like to go for a pint of beer with him but he declined the offer by saying, "No thank you, Mr Tucker, I am not a drinking man myself", and then giving a pious smile before continuing, "although I am not averse to an occasional glass of sherry."

In 1952 I began to study to become a lay reader as I felt God was calling me to do this. Soon after the curate left and he was not replaced, so in fact I had to take charge and run the church with our vicar from St John's putting in an appearance for Sunday morning communion.

By this time Margaret Vanes had found a position as an organist for some church so I was back to square one seeking someone to play at St Hugh's. Margaret told me she knew someone who was taking organ lessons with her tutor and might be willing to follow her. She introduced me to John Vardon, who agreed to do the job, so he came to St Hugh's and succeeded her. I did not realise it at the time but he would become a major part of my life until he died in 2006.

He settled well at St Hugh's and even joined the youth club, but he had a problem. He lived in a flat over a shop in Winterstoke Road near the Odeon cinema and the owners of the property decided to sell up. This meant that he would be evicted. I was worried that he might disappear and once again I would be searching for an organist. A solution presented itself to me that if my parents would put him up at Lynton Road this would solve the problem. I think, all in all, this idea had grave drawbacks.

Number 11 Lynton Road was a very small house and was only designed for a family of four, and there were already six of us living there. There were all kinds of tensions. Firstly my parents' dissatisfaction with each other and me spending a lot of time as a go-between; added to that my own unhappiness at having to go back to work at Wills' after national service, plus I still missed the good life I enjoyed in the army. It was clear that one more person living in the house would make it even more crowded. Despite all this we all agreed to put him up and he put his furniture in storage and moved in with us.

Dad was not a very sociable person but he did enjoy a pint of beer, in fact this was the only time he went out with us. So there were occasions when just John and my father went out for a drink and often Dad's problems and my unhappiness were what they talked about.

My mother seemed to gradually get more difficult and looking back after all these years I think it was mainly due to the bombing and our loss and being made to return to Bristol. I think my father could see his plan of us returning to Lynton Road and picking up the pre-war threads was unravelling. Also, the first signs of the illness that would eventually cause Mother's death were beginning to manifest themselves.

She stopped attending church and when I arrived home after the service she would launch a verbal attack on me as if I was doing wrong by going myself. I've never been given to violence but one Sunday I completely lost the plot and picked up my breakfast and threw it at her. It missed her and the plate smashed against the kitchen door. I ran into the living room and completely broke down.

John was there and fetched my coat and said, "We're going out."

As we left my mother ran out screaming, "Your father is attacking me."

We went for a long walk and John pointed out that this situation had reached a crisis point and that he would talk to my father before the day was out, which he did. He pointed out to him that if it would help, he would leave. My father agreed to this but said that John should take me with him; otherwise someone was going to commit murder!

Eight

Being Independent

In May 1952 John and I moved into an upstairs bedsit in Swiss Drive, Ashton, but within three months we had found a nice three-bedroom flat in Dean Lane, Bedminster. After Mother's initial shock that I had dared to leave home she became reconciled to the new situation and even visited us on a regular basis to clean the flat, for which of course we paid her. At Wills' we were given a weekly allowance of forty cigarettes, which I always gave to my parents, so I made a point of visiting them every Thursday evening to hand them over. My mother was not very good at handling money so I was always purchasing something for them and in no way did I turn my back on them. I even treated her and my brothers to a caravan holiday in Weymouth.

Sadly Mother's health deteriorated; she had always suffered from a skin complaint on the back of her hands, which manifested itself with a mass of watery blisters which drove her mad with the irritation. After using certain ointments the eruption would die down but it always reoccurred. I visited them one evening with the usual allowance and could see that something was really wrong with her. She was shivering and trembling so I immediately called an ambulance, and on being examined in hospital they told me she had blood poisoning brought on by an ointment she was violently allergic to. She needed to remain in hospital for a month before it was properly under control.

At that time I worked with someone who lived in Ilchester Crescent and he told me that his neighbour was looking for a smaller house in the St John's Lane area. By then I thought my dad had realised that it was a big mistake to return to Lynton Road so I mentioned the house in Ilchester Crescent to them. To my delight Father suggested that he and my mother should go and look at it, which they did, and likewise the couple from Ilchester Crescent looked at Lynton Road and an exchange was agreed.

After the move Mother was much better and her relationship with my father improved. Sadly it wasn't to last. I visited them one evening and Mother told me she had a prolapse of the womb, for which she had to have an operation. Then it was not long before she had to have a mastectomy; it seemed as though they were dogged by bad luck.

When I first met John he was a wages clerk for Anderson's Rubber Company in Stokes Croft, but when he had been demobbed he attended a course on men's hairdressing. Somehow, through no fault of his own, he lost his job but luckily found a small shop on Bedminster Down Road complete with living accommodation. As a result of this he moved from Dean Lane and opened a gents' hairdressing shop in Bedminster Down Road. I was now on my own, which I did not mind because I still regularly saw my family and my friends at St Hugh's, and I also got on well with Mrs Hucker, the landlady.

The property John moved into was declared unfit for human habitation and the landlord let him have it for £1.50 per week, but he got to work on it in his spare time and brought it up to a reasonable standard, and a few years later was able to invite me to move in. That was in 1957.

A cottage next to the property had been bombed during the war and a previous tenant of our house had knocked a hole through our wall into the ruins and had then cleared all the debris. The floors of the downstairs rooms were flagstones, so the area became a sun-drenched patio. The frontage on to the road had been taken over as a large advertising board so the patio was completely private and we spent many happy hours sunbathing there.

I went into town one night and saw the bus coming down the hill and ran for it. In those days the buses had an open deck on the back for passengers to get on and off. I ran for the bus and gripped the upright pole on the platform; however I was wearing soft woolly gloves and they slipped down the pole, and as the bus gathered speed I was being dragged along the road, still holding on to the pole.

I didn't panic because I thought either the bus conductor or one of the passengers would see me and ring the bell to stop the bus. However, no one spotted me and the bus gathered more speed and I realised I would have to let go. So I got into as relaxed a position as possible and let go, but the speed I was travelling made me do about six cartwheels across a road junction. Someone I worked with was approaching the junction with his girlfriend and saw me shoot by doing cartwheels, and he was so taken aback that all he could say was that I was Des, his mate.

Her response was, "I'm buggered."

When I came to rest in the road I realised that I was uninjured except that the heel of my left shoe had completely worn away, as had the padded left-hand shoulder of my raincoat, and the white kapok lining was hanging out. The bus stopped about fifty yards down the road and I could see the conductor coming towards me, and I was so embarrassed that I took off and ran up the road. At this point my mate had reached the junction and saw me doing the four-minute mile! He was amazed to see me unharmed and at work the next day.

John came from a very large family with five sisters and two brothers, and the sisters were good dancers. I have always enjoyed dancing so we used to meet most Saturday nights and go to a dance somewhere. The girls taught me lots of different dance steps and it was always a good night out.

Another milestone when we both lived at 103 Bedminster Down Road was when we purchased our first stereogram. It consisted of two units with a range of speakers, which produced very lifelike sound superior to anything we had heard before. Stereo records and units were such a novelty then that you could buy demo records with truly amazing sound effects, such as an express train approaching and rushing past you or even people playing table tennis from one side of you to the other. Music also sounded so lifelike it was just like being at an actual concert.

Both my mother and my Auntie Ada loved to visit us and hear these marvellous sounds, and the good thing about the house was that it had good sound insulation. We often held parties and made a lot of noise but if we apologised to our next-door neighbours afterwards they always claimed that they hadn't heard a thing. Sometimes they also had parties and had a live band playing and we said we never heard anything either, (and the cost of that unit was £120)!

The last winter that we spent in that house was the winter of 1962–63. We experienced the coldest winter since 1947 and the snow and freezing conditions lasted from Boxing Day until the following Easter. We were very lucky because the previous year we had purchased a paraffin convector heater for each room, and also a special one for the sitting room. It was a bit of a bind doing the daily maintenance on these appliances to make sure that they burned properly without making an oily smell. There was a garage round the corner from our house so we bought two ten-gallon oil drums and took them to the garage to be filled.

The country ran out of coal and so people with coal fires were often without heat, and their water pipes froze. My Aunt Ada and Uncle Ewart suffered this for three months and she used to bring washing to our house, and they had to collect buckets of snow to melt to make tea and to put down the toilet and to wash. They used to come to our house for a bath. It was just prior to this freeze that my family moved to their new house in Ilchester Crescent, which proved to be a well-insulated dwelling. The ground in places froze to a depth of four feet and there were more incidences of exploding gas mains. It was such a relief when the thaw finally came.

*

We were aware that Bedminster Down Road was due to be widened and because of that our house would have to be demolished. The council were very helpful and told John that they would buy the goodwill of his business and pay him £700, and also pay us to move, but this compensation was only payable if he opened a business more than one mile from his current shop.

By coincidence there was a lady who had a general store and living accommodation for sale at the top of the road. We went to view the property and it was just about what we needed, with the bonus of a large cellar and a huge garden with panoramic views to Ashton and Clifton Suspension Bridge. John reported this to the council and they generously decided to waive the one-mile clause. As a result of this, a deal was signed and John bought 276 Bedminster Down Road, and we moved in March 1964 and used his £700 compensation as a deposit.

Because it was classed as business premises a mortgage could not be granted so it had to be purchased with a bank loan that had to be paid off in seven years. This meant seven years of austerity for us without being able to afford a decent holiday until the debt was paid.

A couple of years previous to this I resigned my position as lay reader at St Hugh's for more than one reason. Firstly I had always had problems trying to reconcile my own perception of God and Christianity with the information I gathered from the Scripture and the doctrine taught in the church. I felt that what was being taught and practised was a travesty of the real truth as I saw it. Yet on the other hand, one could gather the impression that He was a God of wrath, vengeance and judgement. I was taught at church from day one that from the day I was born a book about my behaviour was being written, and that on my day of judgement God would confront me with it. If on balance I was found wanting, I would be condemned to eternal damnation in Hell. We are taught to believe that God is love, and in his second epistle John states, 'There is no fear in love.' How can this be if an impending doom awaits us if we don't behave as God wants us to?

I do feel also, and have always believed, that God's love for us is so deep and passionate that He came to this world through His only Son Jesus to live and die to pay for our sins. I fully accept that logically there is a price to pay for everything including sin. That price is regret; during the whole of our lives we are forever having a positive or negative way and building or undermining our relationship with God, but for everyone at their time of death or soon after will come the realisation that our time has run out.

If there is such a place as Hell (I would prefer to call it a state of Hell), it is where we find ourselves alienated from God and from all we have loved in life forever. Alienation and utter, eternal loneliness is what I perceive to be true Hell, not fire and brimstone and demons poking pitchforks at us. Even if we do get to this state I believe God's grace will enable us to be rescued no matter how wicked we've been in life. I recently read a book by Archbishop Desmond Tutu called *In God's Hands*, and I found that my views tallied with the views he put forward in his book, so thankfully I'm not alone in thinking and believing as I do.

The second reason was that our mother church of St John's, Bedminster was run-down and eventually closed. I felt that the church forgot and abandoned us at St Hugh's, despite the fact that we had a reasonable congregation and were financially viable. I think the final straw for me was when the diocese installed two Salvationists in St John's vicarage. I have the greatest of respect for the Salvation Army but felt that it was, to say the least, insensitive of the diocese to ask these people to care for the needs of an Anglo-Catholic parish. So for the next thirteen to fourteen years I didn't attend church although I continued to say my nightly prayers and receive communion on Easter Sundays. I think that what I was saying during those years was, "I still love you, Jesus, but I don't like your bride."

The property at 276 Bedminster Down Road was previously owned by Mrs Blanche Tanner, who had a daughter named Marguerite who had recently married David Tipper. I think part of the reason for them moving was that David and Marguerite had purchased a run-down cottage just up the road from Mrs Tanner's shop. The cottage had a large garden and they were living in a caravan in the front garden. The plan was to demolish the cottage and build a new home on the site, for which they needed a lot of extra cash, which Mrs Tanner would put up by selling her house and shop. In return for this the new house would include a room for her so that she could live with them. Apparently Mrs Tanner had experienced a very difficult married life but she worked hard to make a success of her shop.

I'm writing all this because, just after we moved in, John was at the window of the back kitchen, which was at first-floor level, when a strange man appeared in the garden looking up at the window. When Mrs Tanner heard about this she told us that she was sure it was her husband.

Next to the house was a garage forecourt open to the main road, and to the side of it anyone could walk round into our back garden. Next to the forecourt was a large advertising hoarding with waste ground behind, and next to the hoarding was a fish and chip shop. This waste land and its easy access to the back garden was a security risk so we had a six-foot-high chain-link fence built between the garage and the fish and chip shop, with a gate in it and my bike shed behind it.

Quite soon after this was completed a woman turned up and claimed that her mother had purchased a plot of land behind the advertising hoarding and that our fence was denying them access to it. We were polite and promised to look into it but she was aggressive and threatened to take the law into her own hands. Then a few months later we returned home to discover that she had been there with a team of men and destroyed the fence and my bike shed. We called the police but they could do nothing about it because no one came forward to witness what had happened, and in any case it was a civil matter. We had the fence and the shed re-erected but the same thing happened again and so it ended up with us commencing court proceedings, which dragged on for years.

When it eventually came to court it was alleged by her party that in the past our garage and forecourt had been illegally erected on her access path. Fortunately a good friend, Alf Withers, got together some neighbours who had lived in the area for years to come to court, and they testified that our garage had been erected on a wide cart track that had always existed and gave access to the back of our house.

Apparently the frontage on to Bedminster Down Road had been sold at auction to a hoarding company, and at the same auction this woman's mother had purchased some land to the rear of the site with the intention of building there. The judge ruled that the company that bought the hoarding should have left a gap in their frontage to give this person access. So in fact this woman did have some kind of a case, but she should have been fighting the hoarding company and not us.

Mrs Tanner also came to court and testified that ever since she and her husband had bought the property they'd kept chickens on the wasteland and no one had ever appeared to protest or exercise a right of access. At the end of the day the plaintiff had to pay all our solicitor costs but we received nothing in recompense for all the inconvenience and distress this had caused us.

It also led to John having a complete nervous breakdown and hating the place where we lived. The breakdown came in the shape of an acute anxiety complex and the doctor who attended began the treatment by administering a drug which knocked him out for a week, and I was also allowed to dose him with this drug during the week if he woke up.

I nursed him through this for a year and it totally wrecked his business, and there were times when it was Hell for me too. Even as he slowly recovered he lived like a recluse and never went out; he became paranoid about the security of the house. I had to change all the locks and put shutters and bars on the windows and because he had been self-employed there was no money coming in except my wages. It was a nightmare in more ways than one!

As John eventually began to get better he started to potter about doing internal decorating and repairs, and I don't know if there is any significance in this but the colours he used were black, white or red. We eventually began to go out again but even then, sometimes when we were on a bus he would be compelled to get off because he had a feeling it was going to crash. If we visited a cinema he would insist on sitting right by an exit, just in case!

He did make gradual progress. He had two brothers, Sam and Colin, and Sam was married to Pam, who worked as an usher in the Magistrates Court. This led to John taking a job as an usher in the Magistrates Court. Sadly my feeling is that until his death he never totally recovered. I would say he was simply a patched-up version of his old self.

Nine

Mother's Death

While all this was going on my mother was beginning to act in strange ways. For example, on some days she would stay in bed all day for no reason and her behaviour seemed to change, and eventually she became incontinent. Fortunately Father had retired and looked after her. Both my brothers were married so Father and Mother were now alone. For a long time Father had to sleep on the sofa in the front room.

I visited regularly and was very anxious about what was happening, but Father insisted everything was OK. But it wasn't; eventually she had to go into hospital and she had a brain scan. It was discovered that she had a brain tumour, which was inoperable. She was admitted to a nursing home that looked after incontinent patients and one by one all her faculties died.

It was really difficult to visit her because by then she didn't know anyone and didn't respond in any way to anything, and my only consolation was that she was absolutely unaware of anything: to all intents and purposes she was a vegetable. In as far as it was possible she was cared for very well and at regular intervals during the day or night Mother was got out of bed and sat on a commode until the staff were satisfied that she had emptied her bowels or bladder.

Despite their efforts to keep the beds as clean as possible the smell when you entered the home was awful.

Father visited her daily and his visits always included a walk up Redland Hill from the bus stop to the home. One day when I visited him he complained that he was having difficulty making the journey up the hill from the bus stop and needed to sit on garden walls several times to rest. I was also worried that he appeared to be losing weight, but he always claimed he was OK.

It all came to a head when I visited him on a very hot day and he didn't have his shirt on. I was absolutely appalled at how thin he had become and it was obvious to me that something was very wrong. I tried not to let him see how alarmed I was, so I asked him if he had had a check-up recently and he told me he hadn't. I told him a white lie. I said that I had booked myself in for a check-up and if he liked I would make an appointment for him.

When I visited our doctor I told him about my dad's terrible weight loss, and that I suspected Dad had a cancer somewhere. I also told him that when he questioned Dad, he would probably claim there was not much wrong with him. The appointment was kept and the doctor arranged for an X-ray at the BRI. The result revealed that there was a shadow on his lungs.

Another appointment was made for him to attend Ham Green Hospital as an inpatient for tests. This was at the beginning of June 1975. Sadly the diagnosis was that Dad had an inoperable cancer and they told me he had one year to live. They said they would send him to the BRI for a course of radiotherapy and his condition would improve temporarily, but the outcome was inevitable.

I used to visit him at Ham Green, and also met him when he came up to the BRI. When the hospital authorities discovered his wife was in a nursing home suffering from a brain tumour they said he could remain at Ham Green until he died. It was quite a frantic time for me because I was working and trying to visit my mother and my father. I could visit Dad at the BRI during my lunch break.

I felt quite strongly that he should be able to spend his last days in his own home, so my brothers and I met and tried to find a solution, and we also included John in this meeting. The fact was that if Dad was to come home one of us would have to move in with him, and because my brothers were married I was the best option. First I asked John if he was OK with this, which he was, so it was agreed that I would become Dad's carer.

I made them all promise that they would support me, which they did. Then I made the decision known to the doctor and he was very helpful indeed. This was only the second time in my life that I had nursed someone and the first time for someone terminally ill, so I was very scared.

Between us we prepared the house for Dad to come home. He remained at Ham Green until October and then we both moved back home. About that time Ian and Mandy had given birth to their first child and they visited us so that Dad could see his first grandchild, Samantha. Soon after that Ian was sent to the USA to work on a project to do with aircraft. They took a flat in Palmdale, in the Mojave Desert, seventy miles north of Los Angeles, so their visit was the last time they saw Dad alive.

Before the war we had a parrot, which Dad was very fond of, and when I went to care for him another parrot, a blue-fronted Amazon which John and I owned, was brought to Ilchester Crescent to be company for Dad when I was at work. They took to each other immediately and I was regaled with tales of their activities each day when I got home.

Surprisingly Dad's health seemed to improve and he even managed to do a bit of shopping and cooking each day. I organised each evening to give Dad some interest; we sometimes listened to his records, I made a model village and Dad loved to see me play solitaire. My brothers were good to us and paid us frequent visits, as did John.

The first bad shock came in February 1976. I was at work and at about 9am the personnel officer sent for me, and when I arrived at her office she told me she had some bad news for me. She said my father had just phoned and told her that my mother had been found dead at 7am that morning. It was a terrible shock to me because although my mum was in a vegetative state none of us was quite prepared for her sudden death. I broke down completely and the personnel officer held my hand and passed me tissues. When I was sufficiently composed she asked me what phone calls she could make for me, then she took me through to the workroom to collect my things. She also took me to the medical room, where I was given a strong draught of medicine to steady me up.

One incident I shall always remember is that when we were waiting for the lift to go up to the medical department a lady called Jean Brimble came out into the lobby. She didn't actually say anything but simply gripped my arm and gave me a compassionate look, which I shall always remember. I have often experienced situations in which people have avoided others who are in grief, often excusing themselves by saying that they were embarrassed because they didn't know what to say. Jean's compassion to me was an answer to that. It doesn't really matter if one doesn't know what to say, a mere touch of an arm is enough.

I arrived home and I think Norman turned up and he stayed with Dad while I spent the day doing all the things everyone has to do when someone has died. Oddly enough I didn't feel too upset at the funeral; my overwhelming feeling was one of relief that Mother's illness was now over, and I felt that my priority was to support Dad and Norman on this sad occasion.

It was very poignant to be standing by the graveside supporting Dad, knowing that he would be following within the next six months. Ian managed to come home from America, for which I was very glad, and he and Mandy also came back for Dad's funeral. Mother always said she dreaded old age so it was ironic that she died before her seventieth birthday.

Ten

Nursing Father and His Death

After Mother's death and funeral I detected a gradual deterioration in Dad's health; for one thing it became necessary to put a bed in the living room for longer resting sessions for him, although his spirit was still quite high. Sometimes we talked about the kind of things which I am sure, had Dad been well, nothing would have persuaded him to talk about.

I remember letting on that I thought he was closer to Norman than to me, and he asked me why. I told him that I thought they had more in common with each other than I had with Dad. He insisted that neither he nor Mother had favourites but he was especially proud of me because I was his firstborn, and that a strong bond was there and had been strengthened by me looking after him.

His sense of humour didn't leave him either. From the living room we had a good view of Novers Hill, which was a large area of uncultivated grassland. One day it caught fire and as we watched the blaze, Dad explained to me that many centuries ago, in pre-Saxon times, a tribe of warriors invaded Bedminster from Dundry. Their tribal name was the Dingle Boodles and on Novers Hill they fought another tribe from the Chessels called the Gallathumpions. The results of the battle were a bit inconclusive as both tribes retreated, but there was a kind of guerrilla warfare which went on to this present day.

He said both tribes had gone underground but that he could identify among Bedminster people signs that they were descended from the Dingle Boodle or Gallathumpion tribe, just as in the USA you can see when a citizen is of Red Indian origin. Dad also maintained that the Dingle Boodles still held secret initiation rites, like a type of bar mitzvah, in the dead of night when there was an eclipse of the moon, in Plunkett's Vinegar Factory in Braunton Road just off North Street, Bedminster.

Dad also claimed that the Bristol City football club song 'The Red Robin' was really a tribal anthem of the Dingle Boodles. There was also another tribe called the Bumbletooks but they were quite peaceful and remained in Bishopston and Clifton, and Dad claimed that is why the Bristol accent is different to the north and south of the River Avon.

About three weeks before his death Dad developed a fungal infection of the lungs and he rapidly became very ill. He coughed up masses of stinking sputum and although in 1976 there was a drought and a heatwave that went on for the whole summer, I had to keep a fire going to dispose of the sputum. Unfortunately Dad's breath smelled as bad as the sputum and it pervaded the whole house.

I am sure he knew the end was near and when he wasn't too ill to talk he spoke in a manner which told me he was tidying up the loose ends of his life. He asked me if I knew he was fatally ill and when I told him I did he said, "I thought you were the only one who didn't know." I told him that his consultant at Ham Green had told me everything and then Dad asked me if they had told me how long he had to live.

I had to be honest and so I said, "Yes." Then he asked me to tell him and I refused. When he asked me why I told him I was trying to put myself in his position, and in those circumstances that would be the last thing I would want to know.

Dad then said that if I knew he was dying, how could I manage to be so cheerful and upbeat? I replied by saying, "Knowing I was to be with you to the end of your life, I felt it a priority to be cheerful and make you as happy and comfortable as possible."

Dad responded by saying, "You've actually given me the happiest days of my life." I shall always treasure that.

He went into a rapid decline during the next few weeks but he was always asking me to buy him a new clock, which I duly purchased for him from Boots in Bedminster. My brothers were very supportive during this period; in fact, one of them and his wife insisted on me going on a coach trip to London on the last Sunday of Dad's life and stayed with him until I returned. That day out was just what I needed!

We both realised that the end was very near, in fact Dad said that he thought he might last until Thursday, which he did. He was so ill Monday morning that I phoned the department at Wills' and told them that I would remain at home indefinitely, and they were so helpful and kind and told me not to worry about a thing but to keep them in touch.

It was almost impossible by now for Dad to breathe and I doubted if he would make it till Tuesday. When he was able to talk he opened up in a way that was almost alien to him. He said it felt like he was on a railway station platform waiting for a train with his bags packed, and he was longing for that train to come in to take him to Mother and Jesus. He also thanked me for looking after him and said how proud he was of us four sons. At one time it was all too much for me and I retreated to the kitchen downstairs and broke my heart with unashamed tears. At the time I realised that these few last days were infinitely precious to both Dad and me.

I think that evening Norman came over and Dad asked to hear some music. He chose Saint-Saëns' 'Organ Symphony'. Norm and I were both amazed at his choice and we propped him up, sponged his face and gave his mouth a good wash and asked him if he would like a cigarette, and he said he would.

The last movement is just something else. It opens with a thunderous blast on the full organ and the triumphal theme runs right through to the finale. A full orchestra including the organ and piano feature throughout the movement and I would say the whole movement is a grand triumphal march. It was as if Dad was not creeping into Heaven as a sick and defeated man; he was marching up to the heavenly gates and taking them by storm. It was the last piece of music he ever heard. It made such an impression on me that for his funeral I requested that there be no music at all; that wonderful symphony had said it all.

On Monday Dad asked me to get in touch with Auntie Vera and Uncle Fred and tell them that he would like to see them for the last time. In a way that was because in 1928 when Dad was courting my mother, Fred was courting Vera and the four of them became great friends and got about together. One reason was that Vera had a loud, raucous and infectious laugh. Dad told us they often visited a music hall and he usually passed some remark that would set Vera off.

She must have been a godsend to the comedian and on one occasion the comedian interrupted his act and shouted, "What's he doing to you up there, miss?" My father and Fred, when at my grandmother's house, would often insult and challenge each other to a duel. Then they would go into the kitchen and put colanders on their heads and battle it out with pokers from the fireplace.

Dad did ask me to try and make Aunt Vera laugh for him. Anyway, I phoned them and they paid Dad a visit on the Wednesday afternoon. I made Vera and Fred tea and left them with Dad. After they left I went upstairs and collected the cups and washed them up. When I went back upstairs again Dad asked me if I was busy. When I said no he asked if I would stay with him as he was going to get ready.

I sat by his bedside for about an hour and in that time he prayed and talked to my mother as if she was there in the bedroom. It was almost as if he was pulling open a veil and seeing what was beyond. He linked me to Mother and passed messages between us and gradually lapsed into a coma.

Norman turned up and was fully in the picture of Dad's imminent death. Dad developed a fever that lasted all night, and bearing in mind that this was in the middle of a drought and a heatwave, we called for John and he turned up with a cooling fan from his shop. We all three spent the night with him, sponging him down with icy water. He didn't speak but thrashed about in the bed.

Sometime during the night when I was with him he started rubbing his face with the back of his hand and somehow got me to understand he wanted a shave. I fetched his electric razor and shaved him and he stopped feeling his face and I said, "You want to look nice and clean to meet Mum." He couldn't say anything but nodded in the affirmative.

After what seemed an endless night Norman and I decided that we would call the doctor. When he arrived and saw Dad still thrashing about in a bath of sweat he told us that the fungus in Dad's lungs had caused septicaemia to set in. He injected him with something that immediately quietened him down and the doctor left another dose with me to give to the district nurse when she paid a visit at lunchtime. She came and gave Dad a further injection but he was very calm and peaceful and taking shallow breaths about every minute. He passed away at 2.40pm.

I left Norman with him while I went to a public phone box almost outside the house to make some essential phone calls. I must have only been away about five minutes but when I returned Norman was in a bit of a state. It was a boiling hot day without any breeze but Norman said that as soon as I had left the house something like a gale blew through it, slamming shut the open doors.

When we later went back to Dad's room we discovered that at the exact time he had died, the new clock, which I had only purchased a few weeks before, stopped and never ran again. Another thing was that after the doctor called to issue the death certificate, the undertakers arrived. As they took Dad's body away in the black bag, great drops of rain fell on our front garden path from a cloudless sky; it was as if Heaven was weeping at Dad's passing.

Norman and I spent the best part of the afternoon clearing up the sickroom. We ate some tea and then decided to visit my dad's favourite pub, The Miners Arms on Bedminster Down Road. We both felt an overwhelming sense of relief and although we were sad that he was gone, we were glad he was now free from that awful disease and reunited with Mum. We also felt that he said his goodbyes properly and everything that needed to be said had been said, and we felt so proud of him and drank a toast to him.

Above all he died in his own bed, in his own home with his eldest sons either side of him. It was quite an achievement for us all. Norman stayed with me overnight, which I was very glad of. It was so kind and thoughtful of him and he was also a great help the following day when the death was registered and preparations for the funeral were made.

Eleven

The Parrot

Earlier I mentioned the parrot, which I purchased during John's breakdown. When he recovered enough to find a job at the Bristol Magistrates' Court as an usher and I was at Ilchester Crescent looking after Dad, it was obvious that the bird was not at all happy being left on its own all day so it came to Ilchester Crescent and was an ideal companion for Dad.

The bird, which we had named Simon, was quite a character and I had purchased it from a pet shop in Bedminster. I went in there to buy some fish food for our pet goldfish and I spotted the parrot and asked the pet shop owner about it. He claimed it was about six months old and I knew enough about parrots to recognise it as a blue-fronted Amazon.

This species, together with African greys, are reckoned to be the best talkers. Anyway, the shopkeeper got the bird out of the cage and it quite happily perched on my finger, and then it chewed at my shirt button and bit it off. I was completely smitten, and after the shopkeeper assured me it had never bitten anyone I paid him £25 for it plus the cage. I walked out of the shop as if in a dream, as the proud owner of a parrot.

John was delighted with the bird and it immediately took to

both of us. There was only one slight problem, I thought: it was that its beak never closed and it didn't seem to like parrot food. It also appeared to have a breathing problem. We offered it some bits of brown bread dipped in honey and some grapes, which it eagerly ate.

Sadly within a few days its health deteriorated and I phoned the shopkeeper in the hope of returning it and getting my money back, but he claimed it was healthy when I bought it. We next phoned Bristol Zoo to see if they could advise us and they put us in touch with a vet who had a practice in Zetland Road, Redland, who they said looked after the parrots at the zoo and was the most knowledgeable of anyone in Bristol regarding parrots. So we took a taxi to this vet and he said that the parrot had some kind of respiratory infection. He gave him an injection in its breast and it was obvious the bird hated it.

By this time Simon was getting worse by the day and when we next visited the vet we explained that the stress of taking Simon there was adding to its illness. I asked if there was some alternative way we could administer the drug and he said if we could administer it orally he would prescribe it in capsule form. We knew that Simon loved grapes so we cut the grape open and popped the powder inside and he ate it, none the wiser.

The vet made arrangements for me to take the parrot to Bristol University Veterinary College at Langford to check for parrot disease, which is highly infectious and dangerous to humans. Thankfully we were told that Simon had no sign of this disease but was suffering from severe inflammation of the throat and nasal passages. They said that all in all it would be better to have him put to sleep! By then of course we had both become so fond of him that we felt we couldn't give up, so we took it in turns to sleep by his cage each night.

I used to take Fenox drops, which were very effective in unblocking nasal passages, so we put tiny drops of this into Simon's nasal passages. We also put a wire barrier across his cage just below his perch and at night we placed a bowl of Friars Balsam beneath this and covered it with a cloth so that the cage was filled with the vapours. The miracle was that slowly Simon began to improve and I knew he was better the day he closed his beak.

Then came the good and sometimes funny times with him; I have since learned that parrots have the intelligence of a three-year-old and this was proved over and over again. For one thing, there is no such thing as a gay parrot; if you have a male bird it will always prefer women and likewise if you had a female parrot it will always prefer men. This soon became obvious with Simon.

We put his cage in our kitchen and stuck a sweeping brush handle through it so that during the day he could come out and perch on it. On the floor beneath we placed some newspaper and Simon never messed anywhere except on the newspaper, which was incredible as we didn't train him to be clean. However, some of our female visitors took a liking to Simon and despite our warnings would insist on him sitting on their shoulder and then he'd mess down their back, but he never did that to a man!

On one occasion a gas engineer called to do some modification to our cooker and without warning Simon flew into the crook of his arm and lay there with his legs in the air. The gasman was amazed and said it was love at first sight. Another thing that Simon would do when we had male visitors was to cup his head inside their coats and if he found a ballpoint pen he would always remove it, and within minutes he would take it apart and drop it on the floor.

Simon wasn't much of a talker but when I was watching TV he liked to sit on my shoulder and hang on to my earlobe with one of his claws. He would also laugh in the appropriate places and from time to time say, "Coo, look at that." He thought it was his duty to preen my eyebrows and would grip my bottom teeth with his beak and pull open my mouth and look inside.

From his perch in the kitchen he could see, through the open window, the dividing wire fence between our garden and the next-door neighbour's. They had a yapping dog and sometimes let it out into the garden, so when Simon spotted it he would imitate its yapping and it drove the dog mad.

Outside the kitchen window was a wooden trellis and on this

particular day there was a cat sitting at the bottom, staring up at Simon. Then it began to climb the fence and when it got to the top and was about to pounce, Simon scolded it with a loud shout and the cat was so startled that it fell off the fence.

If we were washing vegetables in the sink Simon would get on the draining board and dance with his wings in the air and expect a bath. Although he was now in good health he never took to parrot food and expected the same as us at the same times. As we ate he would look at our plates; then check his own plate to make sure he had the same.

He was absolutely mad about fish and chips and it was amazing to see him eat a chip. He would grip it in his claws and turn it over and over and extract the soft centre; then when it was empty, drop the outer part on to the newspaper. He treated grapes in the same way and you can guess that when Simon came to Ilchester Crescent my father absolutely loved him and found him just as fascinating as John and I had done.

Norman had a beard and the first time Simon saw him I could see he was totally confused, and then I realised why by the way Simon was looking at him. Simon kept turning his head upside down because I am sure that seeing a beard for the first time, he thought that Norman's head was on upside down!

Twelve

After Dad's Death

In the weeks before his death Dad very thoughtfully altered his bank account so that it was in my name. The balance was not a large amount but he assured me that it would cover the cost of his funeral, which it did exactly. He also expressed a strong wish that after his death I should visit Ian and Mandy in America. I said that I would try to do that but didn't have a clue where the money would come from. He said not to worry and the money would be there. Sure enough, during the three months after his death, I cashed a number of his insurance policies and by some miracle there was the exact amount I needed for the trip. John and I both visited the USA late in 1976 and stayed with Ian and Mandy until New Year's Day 1977.

Aunt Ada and Uncle Ewart couldn't come up from Torquay for Dad's funeral but they wrote and invited me to stay with them to recuperate afterwards. So a day or so after the ceremony, which was a fairly low-key affair, I went down to Torquay and stayed with them. They really looked after me very well and it was just the tonic I needed.

Another strange thing had occurred just before Dad died. He called for me one night and I went to his room and he asked me if I could smell something. Well, I couldn't and I told him so but he said he had been woken up by a most beautiful smell, which was still in the room, and that there was a loving but invisible presence with him. He also told me that one day I would experience this myself.

Sure enough, sometime after his death and my holiday in Torquay I was at home and as I climbed the stairs I passed through an area that smelled exactly like the smell that Dad had experienced. It was quite exquisite and more beautiful than anything I had ever smelled in my life. I got to the top of the stairs; then rushed back down to try and smell it again but it had completely disappeared.

I discovered very soon after Dad died that I had a very painful hernia, which my doctor explained was due to lifting Dad during his illness. I visited the council offices to report Dad's death but they told me they could not give me the tenancy to Ilchester Crescent but would let me stay there as a user, but seeing as it was a large family home, if someone in need applied to them they might have to move me out and put me in a flat somewhere.

I talked to John and suggested that I return to Bedminster Down Road with him, but his dislike of his house was so strong that he suggested that I asked to be moved to a flat in the centre of the city and he would try and sell the house and join me. I went back to the council and they suggested that I advertise for an exchange, which I did, and sure enough someone was interested but their flat was on the huge Laurence Hill roundabout, which I was not keen on.

John made many attempts to sell his property but there were no takers because of it being shop premises. Then I received a call from him one Sunday morning telling me that a heavy vehicle had careered backwards down the hill and crashed into the corner of his house, ruining the shopfront and making the frontage above it very unstable. The police had advised him to get a builder there immediately to stabilise the frontage, which as he spoke to me they were doing, and they were also installing scaffolding and acrow props to stop it collapsing.

The owner of the vehicle accepted full responsibility and the insurers told John to go ahead and get it repaired and they would underwrite the cost. Fortunately a very good builder lived near me and came and looked at the job and gave an estimate. We both had a good idea and asked him how much it would cost to move what remained of the front and convert it into an entrance hall and a lounge. Most encouragingly, he said it would only be slightly more expensive, so he was given the job and John asked him to draw up a plan and make a planning application for the job. The council wasted no time and granted permission and the property was made secure and the work began.

In the meantime, I negotiated an exchange with a family who lived in a two-bedroom maisonette at Fremantle House in Kingsdown, and I moved in during the Easter holiday of 1977.

When the work was complete at John's home, it looked really good, and I used to travel from Kingsdown most evenings to help him convert his shop into a lounge. The extraordinary thing was that on the very evening that the work was complete and we were sitting in the new lounge, the phone went and it was someone who was interested in buying the property. A visit was arranged and the buyer offered £12,000 on the spot, and the property was sold in no time without any haggling.

So John temporarily moved in with me at Kingsdown while he looked for another suitable property, which eventually found in Ashley Park.

Thirteen

The Move to Kingsdown and George Fortune

In the meantime I negotiated an exchange with a family who lived in a two-bedroom maisonette in Fremantle House, Kingsdown, and I moved during the Easter holiday of 1977. When the work was complete at John's house it looked really good and I used to travel there from Kingsdown most nights of the week to help John convert the shop interior into a lounge. Another thing that helped was that I had a lock-up garage at Kingsdown, so after his work at court John would come and have tea with me and drive me to Bedminster Down and then drive me home after the evening's work.

I was notified by the BRI that my operation for the hernia would be performed during the summer, for which I was very grateful because by now it had become very painful indeed. In those days after such an operation you were off work for three months to recover, and I must admit that despite the pain, which grew less and less, I really enjoyed the long break.

I liked living at Kingsdown; it was so convenient to get into town and another bonus was that just opposite my flat was the Hillgrove Porter Stores, and to me this was the perfect pub. Kingsdown was quite cosmopolitan and any time you visited it you never knew who you would meet, from an architect to a building labourer. There were also some real characters, and two come to mind.

First, George Fortune; he had done just about everything in his life. In his young days he had worked in theatres as a comedian and he also trained greyhounds in his retirement. He distributed football coupons in the flats and we became good buddies, and I found him to be a continual source of fun. He also had a piercing tenor voice and I knew just how to start him off singing, which I usually did around closing time. All the customers used to join in and then the landlord had a job to chuck us out.

We were such good friends that when George died his family asked me to take his funeral service. I was slightly daunted by this because it would be my first funeral. The undertakers contacted me and told me it would be at Arnos Vale Cemetery. I very carefully prepared the service and duly arrived at Arnos Vale.

There were two chapels set aside for cremation. Chapel A was an imposing classical building for large funerals and Chapel B was a small modern building for small funerals. On arrival I checked the duty list and found I was booked in at Chapel B. I robed up and sat there, becoming more and more nervous by the minute, and then the cemetery manager came and asked me if I knew how many people would be attending. I told him I knew it would be a large number and so he told me to gather up my things and move to Chapel A, which I did.

By then it was almost time for the service, so I stood on the steps to receive the coffin. There must have been some kind of a mix-up because all of the mourners were trooping into the other chapel. I could do nothing although I could see what was going on, and it ended up with all the mourners in the wrong chapel.

The only people who turned up following the coffin were Joan and Pat, who ran The Hillgrove Porter Store. It was the first time Joan had ever seen me in my robes and she turned to Pat and said, "Ooh, Pat, doesn't he look the part?"

And he retorted, "Well, he is the part, you silly bleeder!"

I tried to signal to the pall-bearers to hold everything till the mourners arrived but they misunderstood my instructions and brought the coffin into the chapel with only myself and Pat and Joan present. Suddenly the doors were thrown open and the mourners poured in like buyers at a spring sale; George's immediate family were trodden on in the rush. It was pandemonium!

To utter the opening sentence of a funeral service would have been totally inappropriate, so I simply welcomed them and said, "If George could see what just happened, he would have loved it."

I managed to weave into the service stories of the fun I enjoyed with George and some of his other adventures, and they loved it. They told me afterwards that it was the funniest funeral service anyone there had ever attended. I think looking back on George's life it was obvious to me that he was a very generous and loving man. He made people laugh because it made them happy, and he didn't do it as an ego trip or to take the mickey. He was generous by giving of himself and not by throwing his money around. I tried during his funeral to show mourners that George was the kind of man that Jesus would have had particular compassion for.

Secondly, there was a very tall, thin man called Bert who was obviously gay, and he was always there Friday nights selling eggs. Occasionally the landlady's daughters would take him upstairs and dress him in drag and he would do a take-off of Marlene Dietrich. He also had a wicked, camp sense of humour.

Each year early in December we had a pub outing to Majorca, and of course Bert came with us and brought a wardrobe that would have done credit to a film star. He took hours to prepare to go out each evening but we were all fond of him and took care of him.

Every Friday night two of my brothers and I met at my flat and then we spent the evening in the pub. Then we would all come back home for supper.

Fourteen

Becoming a Tourist Guide

In the summer of 1977 while I was recuperating from my operation I spotted a tourist information trailer in Broadmead, so I went in and had a good look at all the information. There was a man in charge who was wearing a blue badge, and when I looked closely I could see it said, 'West Country Tourist Guide.' I said to him that I thought it was something I would like to do. He suggested I apply to go on the training course, which was run in the humanities department of the technical college on Ashley Down Road. I did apply and was invited for an interview, with the result being that I was accepted for training on the next course, which began in January of 1978.

It turned out to be a very demanding course with two lectures each week on the same night, starting at 6.30pm and ending at 9pm. It was very fortunate that I had moved to Kingsdown because I simply would not have been able to make it had I been living at Bedminster Down. Even at Kingsdown I only had time to rush home, grab a snack and change and be out of the house again in fifteen minutes to catch the bus.

The range of topics was phenomenal, from teaching us indexing of information, filing systems and necessary reading, to lectures on lecturing, elocution techniques for speaking out of doors and preparation for tours, and that was just a sample of some of the subjects we had to study. There was also fieldwork, which took place monthly on Saturdays. This would involve us visiting archaeological sites, cathedrals and public buildings, and going on coach trips. We always carried clipboards and notepads and knew we were being assessed all the time, so if your fieldwork was very good it could earn you credits to offset any deficiencies in the classwork or exams. Miss Karin Cross, our director of studies, was brilliant and although it was really hard work I enjoyed every minute of it. After sitting an intermediary exam in June and passing it I sat the finals just before Christmas and qualified as a tourist guide.

I think the real source of inspiration for wishing to be a tourist guide was a visit to Chartres in France, where there is a beautiful cathedral glazed with the most fabulous stained glass of anywhere in the world. I wandered into the building in the morning and was completely overwhelmed by the beauty of it, but was frustrated by all the information, which was in French. Then I spotted a notice in English stating that there would be a tour in English after lunch.

In the afternoon I returned and joined the tour and the English guide was wonderful; his passion and love for the building transmitted itself to us but he interpreted it in such a way that we could all understand it, and there and then my desire to be a tourist guide was born. I learned later that he was a professor at Bristol University but his passion for Chartres Cathedral was such that every summer during the vacation he stayed in France and conducted tours daily.

Later during my training Karen Cross told us to thoroughly acquaint ourselves with all the information we might need for our tours, but never to lose sight of the fact that we were not historians but simply acting to enable our clients to get the maximum pleasure from being with us and enjoying what we were trying to show them. She said that they would probably forget ninety per cent of what we told them but that they would always remember having a good time with us, and that with a bit of luck, we might have taught them to be more observant and appreciative of the interesting sights around them.

I think this is true of that guide at Chartres; I've forgotten most of what he told us but I shall never forget his deep love for the cathedral or the enthusiasm that he passed on to me. That was really what I tried to aspire to. My true delight was that maybe for the first time in my life, I had discovered something that I was truly interested in and wanted to prove myself good at.

The next thing was to discover a way to put this talent to good use, because at that time Bristol was not really a tourist attraction but rather a manufacturing city. In fact I found out that the majority of existing guides got work through hanging around hotels and touting for work in opposition to each other. I had one advantage and that was through working at Wills'; I was very well known there and had become a bit of a nine-day wonder doing the tourist guide course, and I was even featured in the works' newspaper.

I decided to capitalise on this and in January started doing a series of pilot walks around the city on my own, carefully mapping out about twenty potential walks. It involved a lot of research and reading, which I did until April and then advertised a series of walks to be held weekly if any Wills' employees wished to join me. The fee would be 50p per person, payable to me at the end of each walk. I also undertook to post an advance notice on all the noticeboards stating where the next walk would meet, and to simplify things each walk would commence at 7.30pm and finish at 9pm. Lastly, the whole series would start in the beginning of May and end during August.

The very first walk that I conducted was from Bristol Bridge and I got there very early to do some mental revision and waited. Then the people began to turn up and by the starting time about forty people were waiting, and I must admit I was absolutely terrified. It's one thing to know all the theory but another thing to put all that theory into practice.

Anyhow, I got through my first walk unscathed but shattered. The following day I received many favourable comments and promises to turn up the following week, and I think that each week, as my confidence grew, I enjoyed it more and more and the numbers were maintained throughout the summer. This became an annual event for many years.

Sadly in the end it was spoilt because lots of bars opened up in the centre of the city and drunken yobs made it impossible for me to work there. There was also a persistent problem with beggars so I had to discontinue the city walks.

During the guiding course I had trained to guide in St Mary's, Redcliffe and Bristol and Wells cathedrals, and I did a residential three-day course for Salisbury Cathedral. I did occasional tours at all these churches, so I kept my hand in.

Looking back on my guiding career it was most enjoyable and I think I only ran into trouble once, and that was in Bristol Cathedral. On one of my tours there was a man who was quite objectionable and I sensed he was doing his best to undermine me, mainly by asking awkward questions. The tour was almost finished and I took the party into the south aisle of the choir, where there are some recumbent stone effigies of knights in armour. Some have their legs crossed and some don't. I tried to explain that the ones with their legs crossed were the ones that went on the crusades to the Holy Lands and the rest didn't.

This awkward man demanded to know why this was so, and I really don't know what possessed me, but quick as a flash I replied, "Because, sir, there were no gents' toilets between London and Jerusalem!" My group howled with laughter and that man was silent for the rest of the tour.

At the time I was training to be a guide, John spotted an advert for a property in Ashley Park, St Andrew's, so we decided to go and have a look at it. The street consisted of large Edwardian houses with single bays and front gardens, and the house we wished to view was at the far end of the cul-de-sac and had a small garage at the side.

The front garden was full of rubbish such as motorbikes, TVs, old fridges and furniture, which in itself would have put off most potential purchasers. However, we knocked on the door and were admitted by a young teenager who said he was the owner. As we entered there was an awful smell, and the inner glass door had been smashed and the broken glass just left on the floor.

We were shown into what one would call the breakfast room, which was full of teenagers, dogs and cats, and the room smelled just as bad. The pets had been allowed to mess and urinate anywhere and in the bedroom above the breakfast room the wall was splattered with blood. Outside the breakfast room there was a large modern conservatory chock-full of rubbish, just like the front garden.

On the plus side it was evident that in the past the house had been well looked after. All the walls throughout were covered with good quality washable wallpaper and it looked as if there was a new electricity circuit. There was also a good workroom in the attic and the roof was under-felted. We finished our visit and went back to my flat.

The asking price was about £12,000, which was very low for that location. We both agreed that it looked as if the property would be OK after a long, deep clean. John got in touch and made an offer of £10,000. He was informed that the property had been repossessed by the bank due to a complete lapse of the mortgage repayments.

There was actually a very tragic story. The boy's father was a builder who had renovated the property, and during the course of this his wife had died suddenly. He finished the job and also died, leaving his two teenage sons, and they just didn't have a clue and turned it into a hippy centre. They all moved in with their pets, rubbish and bizarre way of life and that was the reason for its appalling state.

To our surprise the offer was accepted and John bought it for cash, so after having lorryloads of rubbish removed from the front garden and the conservatory, we completely cleared and then scrubbed the breakfast room and took John's furniture out of storage and piled it into the room. It took one year of scrubbing and cleaning before it was fit to move into, but when it was complete it was a lovely house with two shower units and toilets and an upstairs bathroom. There were even handbasins in each bedroom.

John maintained it very well and when he retired from the Magistrates' Court he sold it without any delay or problem for £56,000, which was a good price for a house in Ashley Park at that time. The reason I've written all this is because when John died he left me all this money, which eventually paid for my move to my present address.

Fifteen

Visit to Israel and Conversion

Something was about to happen that would change my life forever. At that time there was a lottery fund to raise money to build a sports centre at Hengrove, and also to restore Ashton Court building. The tickets were sold as scratch cards from a kiosk in Broadmead and cost 25p each. Normally I don't gamble but I bought these scratch cards regularly, regarding it not so much as a gamble but as a donation to something I was keen on.

One day I was lucky and won a prize, and part of it was for me to send my ticket to the city council and it would then be put into a further raffle, for which the first prize was £1,000. So I dutifully sent off my ticket and then a few days later I was notified that I had won the first prize and I was to collect it from the Council House. I was over the moon and told John that I would spend it on a holiday for us both, and at that time £1,000 was enough for a really luxurious holiday.

We discussed a destination and I said that it had always been an ambition of mine to visit Egypt. I especially wanted to see the Valley of Kings and the treasures of Tutankhamen's tomb in the Cairo Museum, and of course there were the pyramids and Luxor. John was quite adamant that he would like to visit Israel, so I reluctantly gave in and went along to Thomas Cook, the travel agent, and booked our holiday.

I remember telling the girl that I was not a churchgoer so I would not like to go on a pilgrimage there. To my surprise she told me that they did tours for people like me and it would be a kind of historical and archaeological tour. This put my mind at rest and so we booked a three-week holiday there.

We flew into Ben Gurion Airport and a courier was waiting for us to get our party together, and when he had introduced himself to us he said he was not a Jew but an agnostic Israeli, which put me at rest. I thought, Thank God we shall be spared having any kind of religion rammed down our throats. That was exactly how the holiday turned out. He was a very good guide and I even think his lack of faith enabled him to be more informative about Israel itself.

Of course the history of Israel especially Jerusalem, is inextricably tied up with the three great faiths which started there. Abraham is also the root of Christianity and Islam, so people adhering to any of these faiths regard Jerusalem as belonging to them, hence all the tensions there. Anyhow, our guide did a brilliant job of leading us and instructing us.

What amazed us was that despite the modern state of Israel being only about the size of Wales it had great differences of climate within its boundaries. When we stepped off the plane the climate was very hot and humid and the whole area consisted of banana plantations. It was a steady climb to Jerusalem, which was drier and cooler, and then beyond the city was the Judean Desert, which was an endless series of small, absolutely barren hills, and very dry and hot. Through the desert ran a road to the Dead Sea and Jericho, which was a gradual descent, and we were told that the Dead Sea is the lowest point on earth, 1,300 feet below normal sea level. It is so salty that you can lie on the surface because the concentration of salt makes you completely buoyant. The most fertile area is a small flatland between Nazareth and Cana; here the climate and soil are so good that anything will grow and flourish.

There is a very high spot called Safed and from there you can look west and see the Mediterranean Sea, or look east and see Lake Galilee. I found Jerusalem on the whole impressive but tatty. The Church of the Holy Sepulchre, with the sarcophagus where Christ was laid and the remnants of the Hill of Calvary on which He was crucified at its centre, is shared by Catholics, Eastern Orthodox and Christian Armenians, who jealously guard their own parts of the building and frustrate any attempt to do any worthwhile restoration work. This means that the tomb of Christ is enclosed within an appallingly ugly stone casing, which in turn is collapsing and held up by an iron scaffold which has been there for decades. Even the sarcophagus itself has a dirty piece of plate glass on top of it. I was glad when I viewed it that I was not an active Christian as I think I would have felt completely disillusioned.

It is strange and sad that the most beautiful building in Jerusalem is the Dome of the Rock. It is not a mosque but a Muslim shrine marking the spot where Mohammed, their prophet, is said to have ascended for his journey to Mecca. The shrine is built on or near the site of the temple. We found that the Church of the Beatitudes, built at the top of the hill overlooking the Sea of Galilee and the site where Jesus preached the Sermon on the Mount, was the most peaceful and beautiful place that we visited.

Anyway, on our last day, in the morning, we visited the Church of All Nations, which stands in the Garden of Gethsemane. The Church of All Nations is constructed around a flat piece of rock, about forty foot by forty foot and surrounded by a low barrier at which pilgrims can kneel and pray. By this time of course all of us on the coach had got to know each other very well.

Up to that point in our tour I absorbed all the things we had seen and experienced in a dispassionate, critical way, but when I entered that church I was aware of the presence of Christ and actually saw Him kneeling on that rock, praying. I was oblivious to everything and everyone else and even the church itself. I fell to my knees at the barrier and felt within me a tremendous outpouring of love towards Him, and at the same time I was aware of my life up to that point spread out in front of me like a huge book or a map, and seeing it all

I was horrified at how petty and worthless it appeared, and I wept bitterly.

Then Jesus actually spoke and said, "I had to let you see all this but I love you and have always loved you since the beginning of time, and I love you as you are, you are infinitely precious to Me."

I felt such warmth of feeling and love pouring from Him into me, unlike anything that I had ever experienced. I remember saying, "I don't know how I shall behave in the future but I know one thing: You have changed my life forever."

The odd thing is that when I got back to the coach John said, "Where did you get to in that church? We looked high and low for you and you made us all panic at your disappearance." Looking back, I think I was gathered up out of time and space and I know that for that brief time I knew the secret of all things, although that knowledge was only fleeting.

Anyway, I apologised to John and tried to explain my disappearance but I assured him that maybe it was a self-induced illusion and if it was, day by day the memory of it would fade and I would get back to normal, and so it was a case of 'Don't panic, just wait and see.'

We visited Bethlehem in the afternoon and returned to the UK the following day but I found that during the next few weeks, rather that that experience receding like a lost dream, it was as if I was on a roller coaster that was out of control and I could do nothing about it. I prayed with an intensity that I had never experienced before and I really began to study the Bible in earnest.

After about three weeks of this I felt that I'd had enough and decided to contact someone to talk about it, but who? I had been out of active membership of the church for so long that I didn't know anyone I could talk to about it all. Then I remembered that in preparation for one of my conducted walks, I had visited and researched the church on St Michael's Hill, known as St Michael on the Mount Without. I was lucky and found the church open and a man was inside doing some cleaning. I introduced myself and asked if I could pay the church a visit with a party on a particular night. The man's name was Fred Miles, and to my delight he agreed to open the church for me.

The tour took place and we entered the church. An elderly clergyman, who told us his name was Vyvyan Jones and that he was the rector, met us and he had rigged up a screen and projector and invited us to view his pictures. The tour as I had planned it flew out of the window and we all stayed there and saw these wonderful historic slides of not only the church but the parish as well. He impressed us all with his knowledge and deep love of his church and parish, and also how articulate he was. At the end of the evening we all thanked him and I think I was so impressed that when I collected all the money we gave it to him for his church. So on the night that I decided that I needed to talk to someone, it was Vyvyan Jones that I called.

He listened while I told him about my experience in Israel and my worries since, and he listened patiently till I had finished. Then he asked me if I had read the story of Paul's conversion on the road to Damascus in the Bible. He said that I had had a Damascene experience, which is so rare among Christians that many of us would give anything for it to happen to us. He couldn't tell me what the future held for me, but one thing he said he did know was that I would never know another moment of peace until I found out what God wanted of me. He said it was something special, and that for a start he recommended that I join a church, because Christianity can only be learned and developed and practised in a community.

I replied, "Well, thank you for your sound advice. I will turn up at your church next Sunday." To my surprise he suggested that it would be better if I went to another church as he said that his was a dying church and would not be a good place for me to nurture my newfound faith. I replied, "I am certain God meant me to call you and attend your church, so that is what I shall do. What time are your services?" He told me that there was a parish communion at 9.30am, matins at 11am and evensong at 6.30pm, and he added that the only service where there was a spark of life was at the parish communion, and with great reservations suggested I attend that service, which I did the following Sunday.

Sixteen

Joining St Michael's

Vyvyan Jones introduced me to John Manley, who was captain of the bell-ringing team and was studying at Bristol University, and he told me that the St Michael's Church tower was the headquarters of the University of Bristol Society of Change Ringers, and that for many years the rector had cultivated a very strong bond with the ringers. John took me up the tower and that began a relationship between me and them which has lasted till now, and in fact I am a lifelong honorary member of the society. The ringers quite often read the lessons at evensong and augmented the choir, and afterwards crossed the road to The Scotsman and His Pack pub, which they regarded as theirs, and I liked to join them.

Vyvyan asked me to preach and to tell the congregation about my experience in Israel and it wasn't long before I asked for my licence as a lay reader to be renewed. My joining St Michael's coincided with the rector's last six months at the church before his retirement, which was very useful to me because it helped me to get my feet under the table and also gave me credibility with the congregation.

There was another reader at St Michael's whose name was Ron Pedlar, but he lived at Mangotsfield so he couldn't really do much pastorally and he could only attend one service on Sunday. His association with St Michael's began when he taught at St Michael's Primary School.

Everything was slotting into place to make me feel really at home at St Michael's, and I regard Vyvyan Jones as a great man and a wonderful pastor; you only needed to tell someone that you attended St Michael's on the Mount Without and if they were Bristolian or a parishioner they would immediately know VJ, as he was affectionately called, and tell you a story of something good and worthy that he had done on behalf of his parishioners.

In conversation with him I discovered that he became a member of the city council because he spent so much time badgering the council office for a fairer deal for one or another of his parishioners that he adopted a policy of 'If you can't beat them, join them!' He got elected to the city council and was eventually in charge of the housing department.

I also asked him what made him become a socialist and he explained that he had spent his childhood in a mining area in South Wales, where his father was a schoolteacher. Quite often there were fatal accidents in the pits and soon after the deaths of these miners the families of the victims were evicted from their homes and were made to camp out on the slag heaps. VJ said that even as a child he was enraged at this injustice and never forgot it. As he grew up and became politically aware he came to the conclusion that the only way to right this wrong was to join the Labour party, because from his perspective this party fought for people like the miners and tried to redress social injustices.

When VJ retired his successor was Leonard Burn, who unfortunately faced two major difficulties. For one thing he was following someone who had been the incumbent for forty-six years and was a hard act to follow, and for another thing the diocesan authorities intended that VJ would be the last rector, and so Leonard was not installed as a rector but as priest in charge, so de facto, he could be sent somewhere else at any time. He was also appointed as Anglican chaplain to the BRI, which took up the main share of his time. As part of the living, it was the job of the incumbent to be chaplain of the two almshouses on St Michael's Hill. One was known as Colston's Almshouse and another almshouse at the top of Christmas Steps known as Foster's Almshouses.

While this was happening at St Michael's I was made redundant from my job at Wills'. It came about because at that time I operated cigarette machines that manufactured 2,500 tipped cigarettes per minute and a German firm designed a machine capable of producing 7,500 cigarettes a minute. It was so much simpler to operate and run that one person could run two machines, making that person's output 15,000 against 2,500, so even if sales didn't drop the firm needed to shed about thirty machine operators immediately.

The terms were very generous; we would be paid a full pension, as if we were retiring at the age of sixty, plus a very generous severance pay. I knew when the offer was made that with my guiding experience I could easily make up the difference between my pension and my wages, so I jumped at this opportunity and retired at the age of fifty.

It was just right because I looked after the services at the almshouses for Leonard and helped him at the BRI, which was brilliant for what lay ahead. The Non-Conformist chaplain was Bill Cobley, who was pastor at Broadmead Baptist Church. It was as if some unseen hand was treating my life like it was a jigsaw puzzle and putting the right pieces into the right places in the puzzle. Leonard Burn didn't stay long and we depended on visiting clergy to look after us on an ad hoc basis.

Another strange thing happened: someone who was a housemaster at Clifton College had been ordained as a priest a few years previously, so he was also the school chaplain. His name was Michael Lane. He retired and visited us at St Michael's on many occasions and the congregation loved him. Someone suggested that he become our priest in charge as a non-stipendiary minister, and the bishop agreed to this.

It worked out perfectly. He was very good pastorally but he had one defect: he was totally tone-deaf and couldn't sing at all. We came to an arrangement that I became a cantor and did all the singing at the parish communion and I also took evensong. We abandoned matins! This worked out very well.

I think you would describe Michael Lane as a delightful eccentric. Later when I met some of his former pupils they confirmed this, but also said he was a mathematical genius. He could be presented with a very complex mathematical problem and would actually visualise the solution just by looking at it.

His wife Patricia also got very involved in the parish and was a first-class host and organiser. She once solemnly warned me never to let Michael near anything mechanical or electrical, and I do recall him getting tangled up in the microphone cables on many occasions during worship, but he was so human and it was a very happy time for us.

Seventeen

St James' Church and Choir Join Us

Ron Pedlar, my colleague, took it in turns with me to conduct evensong and so on my Sunday evenings off I asked if I could ask permission to conduct evensong at St James' Priory Church near the bus station. It is Bristol's oldest church built mainly in the Norman style, and the story goes that when Robert of Gloucester was building Bristol Castle he donated ten per cent of the masonry to build St James' and its priory, and he is buried in the south aisle.

The church was due to be closed but I enjoyed going there and preaching, plus there was a bonus that there was a very talented organist and a good choir; they even sang an anthem each Sunday evening. At this time Michael Lane was getting a bit despondent that the numbers at St Michael's remained at about eighteen for the parish communion. Also, to my dismay, we had an indifferent choir and an organist who only stayed for very short periods. To be frank, the problem with the choir was that due to domination of one or two people and their obstinacy, the choir was untrainable.

The time came for St James' to close and at the time Cyril Mulholland was St Michael's organist. He was a lovely guy who had suffered from cerebral palsy since he was an infant and was paralysed in his left foot and hand. He learned to play the organ in order to strengthen his leg and arm and he coped very well.

The fact is, you cannot simply sack a whole choir because they sing badly, and I know that these problems were not just in my imagination. There was a man about my age who was a music teacher and a fine organist. I approached him and asked him why he had not become organist and choirmaster at St Michael's. He promptly told me in strict confidence that if he did he would have to sack the whole choir and form a new one. He knew realistically that if he took such drastic action it would sink a boat that was already floundering.

An idea came to me that I put to Michael which he jumped at with the rapport that I had built up with the people at St James', and provided Cyril Mulholland was tactfully consulted, I would approach Peter Percival and suggest to him that if and when St James' closed we would welcome both him and the choir to move up to St Michael's. I put this to Peter and he jumped at the idea, and Cyril was approached and he graciously agreed to resign when and if this happened.

We didn't mention our intention to St Michael's choir and I went to the final service at St James'. Then, to our amazement, the following Sunday not only did the choir and organist come to St Michael's but their whole congregation as well, and so, on the first Sunday the numbers at St Michael's jumped from eighteen to seventy people and the church sprang to life. So the potential closure of St Michael's, which was until recently a real possibility, became just a bad memory.

Eighteen

My Vocation and Training

It was during this period of rebirth that I began to think seriously think about becoming a priest. Eventually I talked to Michael Lane about it and he was one hundred per cent in favour of it, although I had the gravest misgivings about being trained and studying for about three years. Then I figured out that I had already shown myself to have the capacity to study in passing the tourist guide's exam, so I thought, Why not? Let's just trust in God and see what happens.

After Michael contacted the bishop I had to attend an interview with Canon David Isitt to assess me and then to slot me into whatever course would be the most beneficial to me. There appeared to be three alternatives. One was to attend a theological college for a two-year full-time course and become a full-time paid priest, but this was ruled out because at the age of fifty-five I was too old, so that left two more options. The next was to train me on a short course to become a local non-stipendiary priest licenced only to St Michael's Church, or the last option was for me to attend a three-year course and eventually to be ordained as a non-stipendiary priest to serve in any church in the Bristol diocese where they chose to appoint me.

David Isitt thought that the last option was the most suitable for me so I commenced training at the Bristol School of Ministry, held in the refectory of Bristol Cathedral each week. Over the three years the course consisted of six modules with appropriate lectures given by tutors from Bristol University mainly, as well as other sources. For each module we were expected to write two minor and one major essay, and as well as the weeknight lectures there were regular weekend courses at Almondsbury Conference Centre and Crodthorne in the Worcester diocese.

Quite soon after the course began I had to attend a selection course at Welling Borough, which was quite nerve-racking; about fifteen candidates attend each selection course and there is a panel of selectors who try to tease out your personality and vocation. These selectors mixed with us for activities, meals and prayers, mainly to see how we mixed with each other.

These are some examples of the sorts of questions they asked: at one of my interviews I was asked what books I read and I replied, "Not many." When I was asked why, I replied that I worked from 7.30am to 5.30pm each day and was usually so tired that I only wanted to watch the TV in the evening and do some gardening. Then they wanted to know what newspaper I read, so I told them it was the *Daily Mirror* because being a tabloid it was handy and spoke my language and therefore I could relate to its views.

On another occasion they asked me what I would do if they didn't recommend me for training and I said that I thought I would probably kneel down and thank God that at least I gave it a go and that it was now all over.

"So you don't think you will appeal against our decision?" they asked.

I replied, "Not on your life, I know that should I not be recommended, I can get on with my own life in my own way."

A final question that the selectors asked me was to describe my vocation to them and I said, "Well, for one thing I feel uncomfortable about it, and about my own suitability and also the uncertainty that might lie ahead, but I feel strongly that for some reason, God wants me to do this and I am not prepared to be defiant, but what He sees in me I do not know."

*

To be honest, on the train back to Bristol I thought there was not a cat in Hell's chance of them recommending me. Imagine my surprise when about three weeks later David Isitt phoned me to tell me I had been accepted.

On the whole, the course was hard graft but very stimulating, instructive and enjoyable. Oddly enough a great deal of what I had learned on the guiding course proved invaluable, especially in how to relate to those for whom you are responsible, whether it be spiritual needs or a desire to know more about the places where I lead my tours. It is a delicate blend of humility and confidence.

Each year during the summer we attended a summer school that was held in Wesley College at Westbury-on-Trym for a one week as residential students. I was doing reasonably well with my studies to begin with but during the second term a very strong-minded woman was appointed as director of studies who was also a left-wing feminist; frankly she turned the course upside down.

I think the students were in awe of her. For example, at the beginning of the first term we met at Bristol Refectory for a get-together party where there were nibbles and sherry, and we informally introduced ourselves to each other and there was a warm party atmosphere. This woman was appointed just before the second term began and I arrived at Bristol Cathedral expecting a similar get-together as during the first year. However, when I arrived slightly late, the students were all sitting in a large, silent circle introducing themselves, and there were no nibbles or sherry.

This woman immediately pounced on me and demanded my name; I thought she was going to give me a hundred lines or a detention! I was a bit defensive and asked what had happened to the party and she countered this by telling me that this was the party, and that the best way to get everybody to know everyone else was to get up and talk about ourselves, to which I countered that a box of party hats and balloons would be much more effective, so I was certainly not off to a good start with her and this state of play continued between us until the end of the course.

The strange thing is that many years later when she was about to leave Bristol, she wrote to me and asked me to have lunch with her. It was a good lunch and to my surprise she said she had enjoyed my mad sense of humour and knew I would do a good job in my parish.

Another thing about the training course was that we were twinned with the Gloucester and Hereford Schools of Ministry and so although we did all our lectures in our respective dioceses, the weekend seminars alternated between Almondsbury and Cropthorne Conference Centre. This was a beautiful old half-timbered manor house situated about halfway between Pershore and Evesham.

The director of ordinands for Gloucester and Hereford was Donald Walters, who had served his title at St Mary's, Redcliffe in Bristol. I was pleased about this because when I was going through my own crisis of faith many years previously, on the recommendation of my bishop, I briefly attended St Mary's as a kind of refuge and Donald was there at that time and we remembered each other from those days.

During our second year of training we had to take a placement for three months in a parish other than our own and I opted to go to Broadmead Baptist Church. Bill Cobley was pastor there and I felt I could learn a great deal from him in that capacity. The first Sunday I went there my heart sank as I knew no one except Bill, but at least he had briefed everyone about me and a warm welcome did await me.

My first doctrinal problem there was Holy Communion, because as an Anglo-Catholic I had been brought up to believe that this sacrament could only be valid if it was celebrated by an authorised priest in a church which could claim apostolic succession, which as a loyal Anglican I felt only the Anglican church possessed. During the time I had to struggle with this I began to know that Broadmead Baptist was truly a church in which the Holy Spirit was working. I therefore reached the conclusion that God was not petty about such things as we were, and with all respect, was not daft!

I also figured that in the early days of Christianity, when it was practised in secret because of the danger of persecution, there were no places of Christian worship so meetings were secretly held in each other's houses and whoever was the head of the household would preside and celebrate and take the bread and wine and bless it. So I was happy to receive communion as a valid sacrament at Broadmead.

Friendships that started during the placements have lasted until now.

Nineteen

*Ordination as a Deacon, Ordination as a Priest
and Ministry at St Michael's*

On the Thursday previous to the Sunday of July 29th 1986, all of us being ordained either as deacons or priests in Bristol began a retreat which lasted until we went into the cathedral. We were quite a large, mixed crowd which included NSMs like me but also candidates who had been through full-time study courses at various theological colleges. So we all went to the Almondsbury Conference Centre and the retreat was conducted by the Bishop of Bristol. It was a good time because our studies and essays etc. were behind us and we could simply prepare ourselves for the great day.

The day came and quite frankly I had an attack of nerves. We all met for prayers and breakfast; then went back to our rooms to put on our clerical robes and dog collars, and for some reason I could not bring myself to put mine on. In the end David Isitt came to my room and gave me a good talking-to and assured me that I was not the first person to get into this state. So I changed and we travelled to the cathedral, but I was still in a state of panic until we got to the west end of the cathedral and I could hear bells ringing. I knew it was the university ringers from St Michael's and suddenly all my doubts vanished like the morning mist.

As we entered the cathedral there was a huge procession and the hymn 'All Hail the Power of Jesus' Name' was being sung, and I felt as if I was on cloud nine. It was a feeling of the utmost exhilaration and awe, which was almost overwhelming. All in turn we made our promises; then knelt in front of the bishop's throne and he laid his hands on our heads. The ceremony was slightly different for those who were being ordained as priests because as well as the bishop laying on his hands, the candidates' friends who were clergymen all gathered round and laid hands on as well.

After this was over all the candidates stood and were presented to the congregation and there was a prolonged applause. Then 'the peace' was exchanged and we all wandered down into the congregation to meet our families and parishioners. A lovely touch was that at the moment of communion our families came to the altar first and we gave them the wine.

Everyone met outside the west doors of the cathedral for photos and celebrations and then I returned to St Michael's Hall for lunch and a party. It is a day I shall always remember!

When the three-year course is complete and the ordination has taken place, a period of four years' training begins when the candidates are actually working as priests. There are no more essays or study sessions but everyone is expected to attend regular seminars, some of which are held over the weekends.

I completed my year's diaconate and then returned to Bristol Cathedral to be ordained as a priest. This is slightly different to being ordained as a deacon because the day before the ceremony, those to be ordained as priests meet to swear allegiance to the queen, who is the constitutional head of the Church of England, and to sign a document binding everyone to observe the thirty-nine articles of faith as printed in the Book of Common Prayer.

Then during the service itself, instead of just the bishop laying on hands as he does with deacons, colleagues and clerical friends of the candidate step forward and collectively lay hands on the candidate, which is quite an experience to be knelt with about twenty clergy laying hands on you. I think that because something was happening to me within a year, plus it was almost the same date as the first service, I was a good deal calmer. Finally at this service I was presented with a complete Bible, as opposed to the New Testament, which had been presented at the first ceremony.

When a new candidate has his or her first appointment it is called 'serving your title' and the new candidates are placed with an experienced priest who will instruct them in the practicalities of running a parish. This should be followed by another appointment in another church to finalise the training. By then the four-year period of post-ordination training is complete and the person is considered ready to apply for a living.

This just did not happen with me because within two months of my priesting, Michael Lane, who was in charge of my parish and under whom I should be serving my title, was taken ill at the cottage called Beaks Mill just outside Bath. He had a severe brain aneurysm and had to be rushed to Frenchay Hospital for an emergency operation. Sadly it soon became apparent that he was going to be severely disabled and it was anyone's guess what sort of recovery he would make.

The bishop sent for me and asked if I would take charge of St Michael's for three months. He told me that he had been advised that any improvements that Michael could make would be within three months, after which point whatever disability he had would be with him for life. He also promised me his prayers and support if I would do this, so I agreed.

Michael Lane made some improvement during the next three months but it then became obvious that he would remain very disabled permanently. He was assessed and Patricia was informed that he had lost about thirty per cent of his hearing and sight, and it was apparent to us all that he lived in a blissful state of unawareness of everything.

Later that year the bishop sent for me again and informed me that after careful consideration with his colleagues, he was willing to make me priest in charge of St Michael's. A ceremony was held at the church and I began my six years of incumbency. One nice thing the bishop did was to licence Michael as my curate.

There is a great wisdom in ensuring that newly ordained priests in the Anglican church serve their title with an experienced and wise mentor; it is not enough to be a committed Christian. Running a parish requires many skills, which can only be learned with guidance and experience. This proved to be the case with me.

Looking back, there was much that I fondly remember and treasure, and I know God blessed me and enabled me to do things at St Michael's that were far beyond my natural abilities. However, it was not a good idea to put me in charge of a parish without having served my title, and consequently I made lots of mistakes.

Twenty

Hospital Chaplaincy

Michael Jarvey, who was the chaplain at the BRI, was an epileptic and tragically he had a fit when he was alone and died. I was contacted and asked if, because of my past experience of helping at the hospital and the hospital being within my parish, I would temporarily take over the chaplaincy, which I did and eventually it was two years before a new chaplaincy was appointed! This proved to be my salvation because although this is truly front-line ministry, it comes with all the drawbacks of parish work.

Some of the patients I visited were very inspirational in spite of their suffering, and I know there were apparently hopeless cases where all seemed lost and yet recoveries came about through prayer. There was a ministry needed there for the staff as well, especially the young nurses, who could be overwhelmed. It is sometimes very difficult to balance the need for skill and compassion and yet be detached from the patients. However, some of it was quite hilarious!

I received a phone call early one morning from the sister of Ward 29. She informed me that she had an elderly male patient with a terminal illness who had expressed a wish to be married. The specialists had informed her that he would only last another twenty-four hours at the most, so could I do anything for him?

I made some enquiries and was put through to the archbishop's office at Lambeth Palace and they informed me that I could perform the marriage ceremony for him provided I had a letter from the specialist confirming the man's condition.

I got back to the hospital and passed this information on and then there was a complication. The patient had been divorced and at that time it was forbidden for a divorcee to have a religious ceremony even if they were the innocent party. Once again I contacted Lambeth Palace and they said it would have to be a civil ceremony conducted by a registrar. So I then contacted the Bristol Registry Office, who informed me that someone would visit the BRI immediately to check whether a suitable place could be found for the ceremony.

By then I had arrived at the BRI to find the groom and his family already there, with them objecting to the wedding on the grounds that upon the groom's death, his new wife would become the beneficiary and the family would be written out of his will.

I talked to the prospective bride and asked her, if I could get hold of a solicitor, whether she would sign a legally binding disclaimer swearing that that once she was married, when she became a widow she would make no claim on the groom's estate, save the cost of the funeral, even if the groom tried to alter his will. The lady graciously agreed to this and I managed to phone around and obtain the services of a solicitor.

When the reps turned up from the registry office they stated that the registrar would need a private room for the wedding. So once again, off I shot and managed to talk to one of the BRI's top admin men, and he agreed to give us the use of the hospital boardroom, which was an absolute gem of a Georgian room on the ground floor. The registry office was happy about this and I arranged with the bride and groom that I would attend the civil ceremony and that immediately afterwards I would bless the marriage.

By now the poor ward sister must have been physically and emotionally exhausted, but I began to see a light at the end of the tunnel and I duly contacted an organist friend to play some hymns and suitable music. The bridegroom was wheeled down from the ward and we all assembled in the boardroom and the wedding duly happened.

I rushed off to the chapel to put on my robes and the organist began to play. Then the ward sister rushed in to tell me that the bridegroom had collapsed and was in no fit state to come into the chapel. She was desperate and so was I, but I told her to tell everyone to do their best to keep him alive and that I would go up to the ward and do a bedside blessing.

When I arrived in the ward the curtains were pulled around the bed, and on enquiry the nurse said it was obvious he was at death's door and I agreed. So I said, "Look, all your other patients knew what was happening and have been agog all day long about the event, so do as I say and pull back the curtains and let's make all your patients part of the ceremony", and the dear sister meekly obeyed.

I duly waited until the groom had rested and perked up a little and then I conducted the service and thought, Damn the church authorities, and apart from it not actually being the legal ceremony, I made a proper wedding of it and everyone joined in, including the Lord's Prayer. I don't know how she managed it but from somewhere one of the nurses produced trays of sherry so that we could have a wedding toast.

That night I slept very soundly and returned to Ward 29 the following morning expecting the bridegroom to have died during the night. I found his bed empty and assumed that he had died, but one of the staff told me that on the contrary, he was in the bathroom shaving. To everyone's amazement in just over a week the man became well enough to be discharged and to begin married life in Cheltenham. Was it a miracle? I may never know, but the ward sister joked that if she had any seriously ill patients in the future she would send for me.

One thing that did upset me during my chaplaincy at the BRI was that quite often consultants would gather at a bedside, pull the curtains round and inform an unfortunate patient that they were terminally ill or that there would be a drastic operation like an amputation, and this was often done while the patient was alone.

I often protested about this and said that there should be a friend, a hospital visitor or a chaplain present at these times. The trouble was that these people had a routine for making rounds of the wards and they would visit each patient in turn. I think, frankly, that they would find it inconvenient to postpone a visit to a patient who was to receive bad news, but nevertheless I protested.

There was an occasion when I was visiting Rosemary's boyfriend in the oncology unit. She was a dynamic member of St Michael's Church. Opposite the person I was visiting was a young farmer from Chard in Somerset, who was undergoing chemotherapy for cancer. He was married with a baby daughter and it was impossible for anyone from home to visit on this particular day. The specialist turned up, pulled the curtain round Jeremy's bed and gave him the news, which I later learned was that his condition was terminal. Then they left him on his own, upset and crying.

Rosemary went to his bed and introduced me to him. I visited him regularly and I found out a lot about his family. At one stage I asked him if he would like me to read to him, and he agreed. The next thing was to choose a book. I prayed about this, and in the hospital entrance foyer there was a free bookstall, and I found Kenneth Grahame's *The Wind in the Willows*.

It was a book I had loved from childhood and I was quite certain that with his background Jeremy would as well, and he did. Most evenings the nurses would let me wash him and tuck him in and then read the book to him until he fell asleep. Miraculously he began to improve and eventually was sent home.

I kept in touch with his family and then one day Jeremy phoned me and told me that the cancer had returned and that nothing more could be done for him and it was just a question of time. Quite soon after his wife called me and said that he wanted to see me, so I got on a train to Taunton and was met by one of his relatives and taken to Jeremy's home by car. During the journey I was briefed about his condition.

When we arrived at his house I was totally shocked to see how desperately ill he was. I took his arm and led him out into the garden and it was obvious from his conversation that he knew this was his last day and that he had been hanging on to see me. He rapidly became so ill that he had to be put back to bed. Then his wife said he was asking for me, so I went to his bedroom and he asked me to lie on the bed with him and I tried to reassure him about death, and he promised that when I died he would be waiting for me. Then he requested that for his funeral, would I wear the clothes I had worn for the visit that day and not my clerical robes?

I said my goodbyes and blessed him and he became comatose, and I bid my farewells to the family and returned home to Bristol. At about eleven that evening I received a call from his wife saying that Jeremy had passed away in her arms just after I had left. I went to Chard to take the funeral and the cremation took place in Taunton.

About a year later I received a call from Jeremy's wife asking for my advice. Apparently she was seeing another man but Jeremy's family were highly critical of her behaviour. She told me how much Jeremy had respected me and she felt the same, and so if I advised her that the relationship should end she really would take my advice.

As a result of our conversation I discovered that the new boyfriend was a farmer and that they loved each other deeply. I advised her that Clair, their daughter, needed a dad as well as a mum and that because Jeremy's parents were still in deep grief they would not be able to think objectively, and that she should go ahead and get married.

Sometime later I once again visited Chard and married the couple in Chard church, and I am the very proud owner of an inscribed pewter beer mug that the family presented to me at the wedding reception, thanking me for all the help I had been to them and Jeremy.

Another patient from the chaplaincy period comes to mind. She suffered from a particularly painful type of arthritis but was in hospital being treated for an ulcer on her leg that would not heal. She was one of those people who never complained and when you visited her she radiated such love, faith and yes, even cheerfulness that a visit to her was a pleasure and you left her feeling she had helped you more than you had helped her.

On one particular day I visited her and found the curtains pulled around the bed and the ward sister told me the consultants were there. When they left I found the poor lady devastated and in tears. Apparently they had told her that the ulcer was not improving at all and was becoming infected, and that their only option was to amputate the leg. Once again a patient had been given bad news without a friend or relative being present to comfort them.

I spent a restless night fretting about this woman and praying for some way of helping her. The answer came very early in the morning. At that time the bishop had seconded a reader from St Paul's parish to assist me at St Michael's and his name was Charles Sevier, and so I phoned him and asked him if he would assist me at the BRI to anoint this lady and he agreed.

So we met at the BRI and anointed her and gave her communion. Astonishingly, within a week the infection in her leg was gone and the ulcer was definitely healing. Soon after she was transferred to Frenchay Hospital for a skin graft and was able to return home.

During the two years at the BRI there were many occasions that gave me cause to be humbly thankful to witness that Jesus' power was still at work.

Twenty-One

More on the Parish, the Bell-Ringers and Organ

St Michael's was a very underpopulated parish with what remained of the houses being let out as flats and occupied by students, and therefore it was a waste of time doing parish visits by knocking on doors. However, I soon discovered there were other ways of contacting people. For one thing there was a very good primary school next to the church and I was one of the governors, and paid the school regular visits and built a strong bond with the staff and pupils.

For another thing, there were many craft shops and even a blacksmith's in Colston's Yard. There were two very good violin shops and I cashed in on this by paying the traders regular visits and just being there to share their concerns. A third thing was the two almshouses, both of which housed communities of elderly people. Each had beautiful chapels and I visited these every week and took services.

Fourthly, the Bristol University Society of Change Ringers had its headquarters in St Michael's Church tower. They rang for our services on Sundays and held ringing practice on Tuesday evenings. I used to join them on Tuesdays and I tried to make the point that I regarded their ringing as a true Christian witness.

At the beginning of each term the church gave a supper to the ringers after their first practice and we introduced ourselves. The good thing about students is that they always appear to be hungry, so it was a good introduction to them. Another tradition was that sometimes in December some of the church choir and the ringers got together and sang carols in the pubs on St Michael's Hill.

I formed such a close link with the ringers that at one of their AGMs they voted me in as a life member of the society. Also on the day of my retirement they rang a full peal on St Michael's bells and presented me with an inscribed watch, and when I am able I like to attend their annual dinner.

The local pubs were also good places to meet parishioners. Our favourite haunt was The Scotsman and His Pack, which was right opposite the church. I called in there one evening and discovered a large empty glass jeroboam on the counter with a label on in red which said, 'For Des' flagpole'. The landlord said they thought it was high time that we had a flagpole on the tower so they were going to raise money for it, which they did, and furthermore the men from the pub hauled it to the top of the tower and fixed it for me.

I remember going in the pub one evening with the ringers after practice and there was a very irate customer playing on one of the fruit machines and winning nothing. He was quite loud-mouthed and everyone could hear him swearing.

There was some embarrassment with this man and his bad language and me with my dog collar on. So I went up to him and said, "Bob, if you want to get something nice from someone, swearing isn't the way to go about it." He retorted that if I thought I could do any better, I should try. I knew I was on the spot so I said, "Seeing as I am a priest, I shall begin by blessing the machine"; then I put some money in and pulled the lever and bingo – I hit the jackpot and a cascade of tokens flowed from the machine, and I scooped them up and gave them all to the terrified man. I am quite sure God has a sense of humour. It was so funny to see the amazement on everyone's faces.

*

Generally speaking St Michael's was flourishing, although some more traditional members had reservations about me and my unorthodox methods and I admit I made many mistakes, partly because I am not a born leader and I know I would have benefitted from gaining more experience.

A stroke of luck came my way when Peter Percival, a retired master at Redcliffe School, decided to move to Hereford, so we had to appoint a new organist named Rob Hughes. This coincided with me becoming a priest. He was fifteen but a very gifted musician and organist. His favourite group was Queen and Rob used to bring his synthesizer to church and dash between the organ and the keyboard, and some of his voluntaries often had bits of Queen's music, which didn't exactly go down too well with the traditionalists.

It seemed to be breathing new life into St Michael's but after a couple of years Rob left and I appointed Reg Gane as church organist. He was an appalling timekeeper but a gifted accompanist and a charming if slightly eccentric man. When he came for his interview and first played the organ for me, he commented that it was a fine organ but in need of some repair. I knew it was very old because our church records showed that it was purchased for the church in 1793, but it was first made in 1540 so it was probably the oldest church organ in Bristol.

Reg said that he would like the job on condition that the organ was rebuilt, which I rashly agreed to. Eventually we called in Roger Taylor, an organ builder who lived in Churchill. He gave us an estimate of £12,000 for a complete rebuild, and in the meantime before committing ourselves to such a large sum of money I wanted to check that the instrument was really that old.

Luckily I was friendly with Malcolm Archer, who at that time was organist at Bristol Cathedral, and I asked him to give an opinion as to the instrument's age and whether it was a worthwhile project to restore it. To his great credit Malcolm agreed to give his services for free on condition that I bought him a pub lunch. He turned up, played the organ and even got inside to inspect it and then pronounced that it was practically a sixteenth-century organ and was certainly well worth restoring.

The next problem was how to raise the money, and someone suggested a silent auction. How this works is that as many quality items as it is possible to get together are assembled in a hall on tables, with a sheet of paper and a pen in front of each item. Then the public are admitted, offered a sherry and some cheese nibbles and invited to circulate and put written bids with their names on the pieces of paper. Then at a given time the bids are collected and the highest bidder goes forward and pays for the item.

That night we raised £3,000, thanks in part to the generosity of all the traders and craftsmen in the Park Row, Colston Street and Christmas Steps area, and those who were members of the church who offered their services as gardeners, house cleaners and decorators. A butcher offered meat, a hairdresser a hairdo and a grocer offered groceries. It was also a great social success.

Although St Michael's Church was not a wealthy church it had many wealthy endowments and I managed to twist the arms of the trustees and treasurer to raise the rest of the money. The job took three months but when the organ was handed back completely restored it was like a brand new instrument and sounded superb.

The final chapter for the organ came about ten years after my retirement and St Michael's was closed and declared redundant. The church house official who was responsible for redundant churches paid St Michael's a visit and to his astonishment discovered that the organ was still playable and fell in love with its tone.

A church in Yougal, Southern Ireland somehow got to know about the organ and contacted the Bristol diocese about buying it. The diocese generously offered to donate the organ free to them, provided they funded its dismantling and shipping to Ireland. It took three months to dismantle and another three months to install in its new home. I was thrilled to be asked to be present at its inauguration.

The Church of St Mary's, Yougal is the oldest Protestant church in Ireland, and although it is not a cathedral it is a collegiate church and a choral service take place in it daily, and St Michael's organ sounds and looks beautiful in its new home.

*

Another revelation to me was to witness how God worked through me and my staff, despite our weaknesses and shortcomings and sometimes our differences. A good example of this was my treasurer. He was not the easiest of men to get on with and in his working life he had been a foreman at St Ann's Board Mills, and the problem was, he still acted as though he were the foreman! Balanced against this was the fact that he was a brilliant treasurer.

This is one of the most difficult of church offices because of the nature of the job. The priority has to be to keep the books carefully and make sure that the budget is not imperilled, especially by a priest, who by profession is a visionary and may not be too practical.

Ken Hippet was treasurer not only of the church but of many wealthy charitable trusts associated with St Michael's, so I had to learn how to, as it were, 'get blood out of a stone' when I needed funding for something.

For example the south aisle had leaked for years and some of its timbers had rotted; in fact each time it rained the rainwater would run down the south isle wall. Vyvyan Jones had it patched up on many occasions but it was a botched-up job, so I badgered Ken into making enough money available to have the roof completely stripped of all the rotten wood and replaced together with the lead guttering and missing slates, and for good measure the builders insulated the roof. Of course I had to work with the church architect George Ferguson and English Heritage, and obtain a faculty from the diocese. The end result was so satisfying – no more water streaming down the walls, and a warmer church.

The central heating boiler was a 150-year-old Robin Hood, and a heating engineer did wonders with it to coax another year's service out of it. I was able to convince the congregation that with some funding we could have a warmer church, so the system was automated with a small computer which delivered a guaranteed temperature when we needed it and ticked over at all times to keep the temperature above freezing. Amazingly, during the first winter with the new heater we enjoyed a warm church for the first time and our fuel bill dropped by £100. Ken was impressed, and I was so pleased. I suspect the good Lord showed me how to get my hands on Ken's pockets.

He and his wife shared a two-bedroomed flat with Dot Clements in Carolina House. Ken was disabled with arthritis so his wife Sis and Dot looked after him. They confessed to me that they enjoyed a game of solo whist but always had to play with a dummy hand. I responded by saying it was my favourite game but that I had not played for years.

An arrangement was made that I should visit them weekly for a game, but I was crafty enough to suggest that there would be a lot Ken could teach me. I admit I was truthful in saying that I was rusty, but we had some very enjoyable evenings and I will concede that they were all good players.

Above all it provided me with a key to Ken. When I won a trick Ken would say, "Now you're really learning from me." It was very funny because if he won a trick he would always brag that his skill had won it for him, but if any of the rest of us won he would say it was just luck. Dot, Sis and I just winked at one another. I'm not sure to this day if you could call that pastoral work but then Jesus taught his disciples to be as innocent as lambs and as wise as wolves.

Another great character at church was Rosemary Thorn; she was a dynamic character and a good leader and together we founded the Sunday club. The idea was that parents who brought their children could leave them at the parish hall, where the Sunday club began fifteen minutes before the parish communion, and they would stay there on some project organised by Rosemary and her helpers and then they would troop into church in time for the offertory and main service. It really did work well for some time but Rosemary's helpers complained that she was treating them just like the children.

But we had lots of good times! I remember being asked to do *Thought for Today* on Radio 4 but they wanted me to send a tape recording to see how my voice came over. I did this, but there was a fault with my machine and the playback was too slow. Fortunately

Rosemary lived almost next door to me in Fremantle House so I asked her if I could use her equipment to make the tape.

I visited her flat and decided to make another recording. The difficulty was, she completely took over and ordered me to sit down. Then as we started to record she ordered me to say, "Good morning, listeners", and what started me off was that she grabbed a candlestick and thrust it in front of me like a microphone. I don't know why but I cracked up and burst out laughing so much I could not continue.

Then Rosemary played back what I had recorded and we both laughed. When we calmed down she decided to have another go, but this was fatal. Every time we attempted to record we laughed more hysterically until in the end we had to give up. I eventually managed to make a recording and submitted it and did *Thought for Today* for a couple of years.

Rosemary and her fiancé Stuart approached me about being married but unfortunately she had been divorced so they asked if I would simply bless their wedding, which I agreed to, but after much thought, I talked to them and said that in my view of her Christian sincerity, as a wedding gift, I would give them a full wedding ceremony. They were overjoyed and a very low-key ceremony was performed at the registry office, but later we held a full ceremony with all the trimmings.

When I met Father Austen Masters during the second summer school we took to each other immediately, partly because he had a wonderful sense of humour and he belonged to a community of priests based in Yorkshire at a place called Kelham. This rang a bell with me because in pre-war days, the Kelham Fathers ran St John's parish in Bedminster. The aim of the order was to educate young men who had a vocation to the ministry but lacked the educational qualifications.

He became my spiritual advisor and it was due to his being chaplain at Clewer that I began to visit the sisters regularly and to care for them when Austen was away. His advice was sound and practical but often very funny. He once told me that there were two kinds of priests: those who had nervous breakdowns and those who give them to others. He told me to make sure I was in the second category.

He also told me that I would find the Devil somewhere in any congregation that I ministered to, but that I shouldn't worry as it goes with the job and happens to everyone. He also advised me to cultivate a friend, preferably not a member of my church, whom I could really trust and use as an emotional punchbag.

Twenty-Two

Alec Rose

I found someone like that at the beginning of my ministry at St Michael's. His name was Alec Rose. He was certainly not a paid-up member of the church but he was highly intelligent and had a good sense of humour. At our time of meeting he had gone through essxaaxa traumatic divorce and lost his business and home, and was trying to make a fresh start by studying sociology at Filton College.

I invited him to my ordination and as a present for me he cleared and dug up a very large border outside the main gate of the churchyard. The thing that really drew us together was the St Michael's records. They were complete, still stored in the vestry and dated back to the early sixteenth century. Once I became priest in charge I gave him access to the records which, over a long time, he carefully inspected and took reference notes for me, which I found fascinating and useful.

For example, St Michael's had three public entrances: the north and south doors, both at the west end of the church, and the western tower door. The purpose of these three doors was to segregate the wealthy pew-paying members from the hoi polloi who could not afford such a luxury. The tower door gave direct access to the nave but the north and south doors did not and were connected by two staircases to the gallery at the west end, and parish beadles were on duty with heavy staves with brass knobs on to make sure no one from the gallery got down to the church except under their strict supervision – that is, for occasional communion and baptisms.

This sheds a light on what eighteenth-century Anglicanism was like. At that time it was obligatory legally for all parishioners to attend their local church weekly, and there was something that you could describe as a parish police force to enforce it. Another thing I learned from the records was that if anyone wished to move from one parish to another it was required that they got permission from their vicar, stating that they were earning income and would not be a burden on the parish where they intended to move.

Another scandalous practice, which we discovered written in the parish minute book, was that the church maintained a wheelbarrow, the purpose of which was that when anyone living in poverty died, they would put them in the wheelbarrow and tip them over the boundary into an adjacent parish so that the parish where the corpse was found would bear the cost of that interment.

I could write a book just on St Michael's records but it is truly an insight into how the Church of England was in the eighteenth century, and it is quite easy to see how Non-Conformist churches proliferated and were loved by the working classes.

At the time that I got to know Alec I was working as an usher in the family division of the Bristol Crown Court as well as being priest in charge of St Michael's. Ironically, as well as embarrassingly, I looked after the same judge whose court Alec's divorce went through. What I knew, but what Alec could not understand, was that in the domestic court the judge sits without a jury but the decision of the judge is not made in isolation. They all rely on reports written for them by court officers, who visit and assess what action should be taken and which parent should be given custody of the children and what process would be granted to the other party, and I think that one needs the wisdom of Solomon to do this job. These people are experts and no judge in their right mind would ignore their reports and advice. However, you try and explain that to an aggrieved partner in a divorce case.

There was one occasion in which I was able to help Alec. I was sufficiently respected in the courts to have the ear of the officers who made the reports and I knew the person who had done the reports in Alec's case. So I asked another officer if, in confidence, she would go through Alec's file and see if he was entitled to any access. She did this for me and wrote to his daughter's school telling them that he was entitled to see her reports, which until then had been denied him.

On another occasion we were both in the local pub and Alec asked me to, in a minute, discreetly look around, explaining that I would see his ex-wife sitting with someone. I did as he said and spotted her, and the person she was sitting with was obviously a thug and they were both there to provoke Alec. On a previous occasion he had told me this had happened before.

I implored Alec not to react but to go outside and wait for me, which thankfully he did. I then went to the landlord and explained the situation, told him who they were and asked him to tell them who I was and that if I saw them in the pub again I would report it to the courts. The landlord was very good and told them to leave immediately and not visit his pub again, and it worked because she never bothered Alec again.

Twenty-Three

St Michael's Traditions

There were some interesting events that took place annually at St Michael's. The oldest tradition dated back to the fourteenth century and its beginnings are recorded in an old council record book. This states that upon the election of a new mayor, this person, together with the alderman, shall solemnly process to St Michael's on the Mount Without, there to hear a homily delivered by the rector and afterwards to take cakes and ale with him, and we still did that while I was there.

Another tradition was that on the nearest Sunday to St David's Day a sermon would be preached by candlelight. This started in the eighteenth century when a couple came to Bristol from Wales and settled in St Michael's parish, and they made a fortune here and so they paid for this ceremony in thanksgiving. The practical reason they did this was because in those days it was too expensive to light a church to hold evening services during winter, so it really was a beautiful treat for St Michael's parishioners to attend this lively service. When I was in charge I brought in a tradition of singing hymns with Welsh tunes at this service, and some who could speak Welsh recited the Lord's Prayer in Welsh.

Until the eighteenth century it was the duty of the newly elected church wardens, immediately after being elected at Eastertide, to provide a feast for the poor at considerable expense to themselves. Understandably no one wanted to be a church warden with this onerous and expensive liability, so the same good people who paid for the candlelight sermon paid for this feast annually and left a fund for it to continue in the future.

After the Poor Law was enacted in the nineteenth century the feast was deemed unnecessary and so it was changed. A special kind of a bun about nine inches across was baked and distributed to the children of the parish on Easter Tuesday after a short service in church.

The almshouses at the top of Christmas Steps have a beautiful medieval chapel with a lovely stained glass window by Patrick Pollen, which was installed in the 1960s. It depicts the three wise men visiting the Christ child and presenting Him with gold, frankincense and myrrh, and the chapel is uniquely dedicated to the three kings of Cologne. Because John Foster, who founded the almshouses, was a mayor of Bristol and also an importer of salt, he regularly visited Salzburg to buy these precious commodities and import them to the UK.

On his journey he visited Cologne Cathedral and saw a beautiful shrine, which is still there today and contains, wrapped in silk, bones that are said to be the bones of the three wise men. He was so impressed by this that he paid for the almshouses and chapel to be built. He dedicated the chapel to the three kings of Cologne. When I was in charge of St Michael's I began a tradition of holding a candlelight communion service on the feast of Epiphany, the old Christmas Day, when we celebrate the visit of the three wise men to the Holy child.

Alas, the almshouses have now been sold and are turned into apartments and the chapel is closed, which is very, very sad.

Twenty-Four

David Holloway, My Last Day at St Michael's,
and Westminster Abbey

One other thing happened to me when I was at St Michael's. The bishop sent for me and explained that one of his clergy had suffered from a nervous breakdown many years previously but was gradually getting better. The bishop felt that this man, David Holloway, would now benefit from being introduced very gently back into parish life. He asked me if I would be willing to take on David as my curate, but it had to be on the understanding that I would be sensitive to his needs and not just regard him as an aid to my work.

I agreed to this and met David and told him that there was a pulpit and an altar in the church that I would be happy for him to make use of at any time, and for him to attend church or stay away depending on how he felt. This arrangement worked well and he often brought his wife Susie and his parents, who also lived in Bristol, to church with him. He improved to the extent that he became prison chaplain at Horfield Prison and he eventually became well enough to accept the living at St Gregory's. He stayed with us until I retired and for my last Sunday at St Michael's I chose the Day of the Candlelight Sermon. We held a tea in the parish hall in the afternoon, during which I was presented with a dining table and chairs by the congregation, and a very fine blue glass fish with the artist's name on its base by the local traders in Park Row.

Looking back on those years at St Michael's I find it quite easy to remember the things that I achieved materially, mainly the restoration of the south aisle roof and the organ, and with Alec's help, completely renovating the tower entrance to provide a foyer upon entering the church. But I am not at all sure about my tenure as a parish priest. I think God alone must be the judge of that.

At my last service Edwin Morris, who was the rural dean and rector of St Stephen's city, spoke very kindly to me and invited me to join him at his church and I took up his offer. Before I retired the sisters at Clewer were dropping in number to the extent that the convent property was sold and they moved to a new home just outside Oxford. Austen Masters retired and was replaced by Lister Tonge, who was a much younger man, but I continued to visit them. Lister was away and I was staying there looking after the sisters, and at supper Mother Superior told me that Lister had returned for an overnight stay unexpectedly and would like to see me. So after supper I went to his house and enjoyed a nice evening with him. During the evening he suddenly asked me if I might consider becoming a chaplain at Westminster Abbey.

I was totally taken aback and I think I said, "Lister, that would be completely out of my league." He replied that this was one of the jobs he did in London and that he would not have suggested it if he was not sure I could do it. He then went on to explain the details of the appointment. He said there was a total of fifty-two chaplains who took it in turns and one week each year went to the abbey and resided there. They did daily duties in the church from about 9.30am till evensong at 3.30pm.

The actual remit was slightly vague but you were expected to robe in a cassock, wear a red abbey waist sash and a badge with 'Chaplain' written on it, and be present in the church to meet anyone's spiritual needs and to talk to them or listen to them and maybe pray with them. The chaplain was also expected to use the choir pulpit once an hour and was given one minute or at the most two to call people to order and generally to remind them that Westminster Abbey was much more than just a top tourist attraction. The chaplain was also expected to celebrate a lunchtime communion twice a week in the nave, at which usually about 150 worshippers attended.

To assist the chaplain there was a staff of vergers and also a band of marshals dressed in royal red gowns, who were there to steer people around and look after safety etc. Having listened to this I agreed to accept the job if it was offered me and so Lister said he would put my name forward, and I was offered the post and did my first duty the following year in Ascension Week.

At the time of my retirement, the dean of Bristol Cathedral, the Very Reverend Wesley Carr, had talked to the bishop about his wish to organise the guiding in the cathedral properly as befitted the most important church in Bristol. The bishop, knowing I was a Blue Badge Guide, recommended me for the job and so I got in touch with the dean and gradually built up a team of well-trained guides which has survived until the present day.

Some years later the city began to organise Open Doors Day annually. There were free leaflets issued giving a trail of places to visit and how best to get to them, and naturally the cathedral was included in the trail. I made sure there were about fourteen fully trained guides on duty at given spots around the cathedral with enough written information to interpret in detail the area they were in to the visitors. Each of these spots was marked with a large number that everyone could see and on entry to the cathedral each visitor was greeted and advised, if they had time, to look for the numbers and follow the sequence around the building. To save the guides getting bored they changed their positions each hour and spare guides made sure everyone had a toilet and refreshment break. The system worked like magic and many of our visitors complimented us and said that in the entire trail, the cathedral was by far the best-organised site.

By happy coincidence Wesley Carr became dean of Westminster just before I started my chaplaincy there, and Westminster Abbey was an amazing place to be. At times you could almost walk on the heads of visitors. It presented all sorts of different challenges at different times. I think such a vast religious place gives the visitors the opportunity to open up just because they knew there would be no follow-up; just a listening ear.

A small private chapel under the south-west tower was reserved for the chaplain's use to give him a place to take anyone who wished to speak to him privately, but the marshals kept a careful watch in case a weirdo gave trouble, though thankfully this did not happen to me.

I think maybe the funniest thing that happened to me at the abbey was when a boy pulled on my cassock and said, "I know how old God is." Towards the west end of the nave there are two icons, one of our Lord on the left and one of the Virgin Mary on the right. In front of each picture there is a candle stand for votive candles and many visitors stop there and light a candle, so in front of each icon there are a lot of candles burning. When I asked the boy how he had worked out God's age he simply replied that he had counted all His birthday candles!

One day Wesley Carr asked why didn't I bring a party of visitors from Bristol and give them a tour of the abbey? So I took him up on his offer and when we reached the abbey he was waiting to greet us wearing his ceremonial robes, and made sure we had VIP treatment. I did about six years of chaplaincy duty at the abbey and then made way for someone else, but I was so glad to have had such an experience.

Twenty-Five

John's Final Years

Just before my own retirement John accepted retirement from the Magistrates' Court, and with my permission sold his house at Ashley Park and moved in with me. I have to state that from the beginning he was not in good health. The thing that happened to set in motion a train of events that led to his death was what ought to have been a minor operation.

It was a condition known as Dupuytren's contracture, which had been brought about by his occupation as a men's hairdresser and using scissors. This caused his little finger to be bent double and he couldn't straighten it, and it was very inconvenient. The operation would involve cutting open the palm of the hand and wrist and opening the sheath that encased the tendon to the little finger, enabling it to be straightened.

John's own doctor recommended that due to the condition of his lungs because of many years of heavy smoking, he should have a local anaesthetic. The hospital ignored this advice and gave him a general anaesthetic. Sadly, although the operation was a complete success it triggered off a series of lung infections and from then onwards he seemed to be in and out of hospital all the time.

We visited the BRI for regular check-ups and X-rays and one day the doctor decided that John needed a full scan. This took place and when we went back to get the results we were told it was an inoperable lung cancer and terminal. This was an awful shock, and so we went to the hospital cafe and it was there I promised to take care of him until he died. This was in June 2005 and he died in January 2006, four days after his eightieth birthday.

Although he had the same disease as my father, in his case it took a completely different course. For one thing he became bedridden quite early and he developed an allergy to light. He was also adamant that he did not want any visitors. I personally think it was a matter of pride. He had always been very particular about his appearance and he was very realistic about the toll that the cancer was taking on him.

There were occasions when it was necessary for me to leave him on his own, either to perform my church duties or to go shopping, and so I purchased two basic mobile phones and his was programmed so that in emergency he could contact me and I could get a taxi home immediately.

The authorities supplied him with a special bed with a pump that kept the mattress on the move to prevent bedsores. I also purchased silk boxer shorts and used baby wipes for the same purpose, and this was totally effective. Part of nursing anyone with this condition is to try and hit the right balance and to keep their spirit up without overdoing it, and to watch and nurse someone you've known for a great many years being killed by this devilish disease. I also think your life has to be totally centred around the patient and everything else must take second place.

It was a weird experience to leave the flat and go shopping and mix with people who appeared to be living 'normal' humdrum lives while this awful thing was happening in my flat; it was quite surreal. As John became worse I feared that he might need the kind of care that was beyond me and so I contacted Vanessa Stevenson, who was a member of St Stephen's Church and a trustee of Bristol Municipal Charities, who had recently opened a brand new nursing home at Henbury.

She kindly took me there and I took many photos of the interior and then I showed them to John. Vanessa also told me that if and when it became necessary she would see that he was admitted there. However, he pleaded with me not to send him there and I promised that only if and when he requested this would he go there. I told him the flat was his home and he could stay there as long as he wished. Sadly his condition continued to deteriorate and he needed more and more attention.

His eightieth birthday drew near and he asked me to cut his hair. I've tried my hand at many things but I felt that if I did this he would look worse after I had finished with him. I used to get my hair cut by a nice young lady in Colston Street, and I talked to her about my problem. She said she would be willing to come to the flat and cut his hair there on his birthday, Sunday January 15th 2006. She turned up quite early and we propped him up in bed for his haircut.

After she left John said to me that we could not go on like this, and then asked if I could get him into a nursing home. I agreed but said, "I will only do this if you are absolutely sure this is what you want, because once I set the wheels in motion there is no turning back." He agreed and so I phoned Vanessa and she made enquiries and discovered that a room was available and they could take John immediately.

I told him I was informing his sisters and brothers and asked them to visit him. Although neither of us mentioned the fact, I am sure we both realised that the end was near. The ambulance was called and I was slightly annoyed that when they discovered that it was a private nursing home that they were taking him to, they refused to take him and we had to go there by private ambulance.

The room was really nice and everyone was really helpful. They also provided me with a mattress so that I was able to sleep in the room. John's family were very good and paid him daily visits and were with him most of the time. This freed me to have a break during the day and to attend to things at the flat and St Stephen's, where my two years' interregnum was ending.

John was daily slipping away from us and was constantly calling to his long-dead mother and father. People from St Stephen's were very good and came in every evening and brought me supper. Sam, John's younger brother, was quite horrified at his condition and said to me that if he had a pet dog in this state he would have it put down.

On Thursday January 19th there were family visitors all day until 8.45pm when they all had to leave, and so I went to the entrance and saw them off. When I returned to his room at 8.50 John had quietly passed away. I had a notebook on me with all the phone numbers of everyone to be contacted and so I went to the charge nurse's desk and she said she would make all the necessary phone calls.

Then shock set in and I completely broke down, and at just the right time Peter and Annette Marshall turned up and were marvellous in consoling me. There was also a young reader from Christ Church who turned up, whose name I do not remember. He had visited during the week and developed an affinity with John, who had asked him to conduct his funeral.

Vanessa asked him to stay with me until the undertaker came for John and when everything was finished to take me to Vanessa's, where she had prepared a room for me. I must have been exhausted because I slept soundly and then Vanessa prepared a lovely breakfast for me. She was an absolute godsend, driving me around the city to register the death and visit the undertakers. It's at times like this that you realise the value of true friends.

Although this was a very sad time I had the consolation of knowing we had said proper goodbyes to each other and so realistically there could be no regrets as he was now released from that awful disease. On the day of his funeral we met early in St Stephen's common room for a snack before the service and there was a large number of people who attended. Sam and I followed the coffin as principal mourners and there was a burial at Canford Cemetery, followed by a family lunch at the community hall in Greystoke Avenue.

The next day I travelled down to Torquay and stayed with my Aunt Ada and Uncle Ewart for a complete rest.

Twenty-Six

Alice Grimshaw

Alice Grimshaw joined St Michael's Church in 1980. Previous to this she had attended St Matthew's Church, Kingsdown. She must have attended there when it was a fairly quiet church with a mainly elderly congregation, quite small in numbers. Then it became charismatic and changed dramatically. It attracted a large congregation of mainly young people and I imagine it became too much for her to cope with.

At that time Dot Clements, who was St Michael's PCC secretary, lived alone in a two-bedroom flat in Carolina House on the fourth floor, and Alice lived in a one-bedroom flat on the second floor. Alice must have complained to Dot about her wheeziness at St Matthew's and so Dot suggested that she give St Michael's a try, which she did and this is how I met her. At that time she was sixty-seven years old and our church suited her to a T.

She was a person who, without being pushy, made friends easily and because of her honesty and loyalty, kept them for life. I took to popping in on her for a chat and a cup of tea and eventually she showed me old photos from her childhood. She told me she was born in Manchester and was an only child. Quite early on in her life her father died and then Alice's mother married again to a man who turned out to be a bad lot and regularly beat Alice and her mother.

To escape him they fled to Bristol and lived in Jacob Wells Road, but sadly one day her mother was run over and killed by a horse and cart and Alice, at a very young age, was destitute. To survive she had to find a job and such education as she had came to an abrupt end. However, she found work as a cleaner at Bristol Children's Hospital and worked there until her retirement at sixty-five years old.

She didn't learn to read or write properly and lived all her life with this disability, and God only knows how she did it and furthermore, made a success of it. She was never self-pitying or bitter about it. The way she lived was a triumph over disaster. She sought out people she could really trust in her social and working life and even in her shopping, where she handed over her purse for them to take out the necessary money and give her the right change.

I think what she lacked in education she more than made up for in intelligence. Many people cannot read or write and are ashamed of it and so try to keep it secret, but Alice didn't do that. She was a first-class judge of character and her instincts never let her down.

When I got to know her she always shopped for food at Marks & Spencer's and went to the same checkout each time and handed over her purse to the same lady who understood Alice's plight and dealt honestly with her. The stores in Broadmead Shopping Centre which she frequented regularly were Marks & Spencer's, Kemps the jewellers, Debenhams, House of Fraser and the Yorkshire Building Society.

Whatever shops she visited, she took gifts of cake and had coffee and a chat with the assistants. When she received her pension she always visited the building society and deposited cash in her two accounts, one for long-term and maximum interest and the other current account for her day-to-day needs. She was so well known there that a special chair was reserved for her.

She also got to know an assistant in Debenhams so well that Alice would order an item of clothing without ever seeing it and the girl knew Alice's size and what would suit her and reserve it for her. She also paid a monthly visit to the House of Fraser where she had a manicure, and there were coffee and cakes all around. Alice also paid a weekly visit to the hairdresser in High Kingsdown for a shampoo and set and regular perms. She frequently visited Kemps the jewellers and paid money in regularly until there was enough to buy something for herself or one of her friends.

Every day she packed a picnic meal for lunch and in the summer ate it in Castle Park or found shelter if the weather was bad. She also regularly cooked meat and two veg for her evening meal and her flat was immaculate; this paints a picture of a lady who was incredibly well organised and loved. She was generous to a fault but her real gift was that she gave of herself one hundred per cent.

As I grew to know her more I made more frequent visits, and always dealt with her post and bills etc. and did any odd jobs such as cleaning windows for her. She never did master the art of changing a duvet. I tried to kid her into going inside the cover and promised to pass the duvet in to her, but she did not wear it.

Sometimes she came out with some very funny words. For instance she had to visit the BRI and she confided in me that they kept her in the cuticle a long time! Outside her sitting room window was a large patio about fourteen feet square and she referred to it as her boscany. In this sense she was very much like my mother, who accused two smart young men of being Joanna's Witnesses.

I would usually visit Alice in the afternoons and she always bought me a trifle from Marks & Spencer's. Once a year she would visit Cheddar and go to a 'pick your own' farm and bring back masses of strawberries for all of us. I gradually took over the cultivation of her patio and each year she would give me about £50 to go to a garden centre and buy geraniums, petunias and other bedding plants, which I then planted out in boxes and containers for her.

She had a good Christian faith despite never being able to read the Bible and she never spoke ill of anyone. One afternoon I was with her and she told me she had been mugged on the way back from the hairdresser. I was horrified and asked her what she did and she told me that she hit him with her handbag and told him to bugger off, and she said he fled.

Usually sometime in September when I visited her each week, she had got ready Christmas presents for her various friends and I had to wrap a few each week. After she retired from the children's hospital she did cleaning for a number of clients in Kingsdown and Clifton and she would give presents to all these people and their families. She was very generous to me and often brought me things which she knew I liked.

Alice was quite unconventional in many ways. For example, in one part of the Bristol University campus there was a beautiful Georgian house and it was surrounded by parkland, which was public. In the summer Alice used to go there during the day and lie on the grass in her swimming costume sunbathing, despite all the students milling around.

Each Christmas she would book into a hotel just off Oxford Street in London and travel there on her own, and apparently she was well known and loved there. Eventually she became too frail to do this and so after John died I took her to Torquay at Christmas and the following year to Plymouth. Sadly the visit to Plymouth was a bit of a disaster because the staff at the hotel found her in her nightclothes wandering round the corridors and she had to be led back to her room. She also fell down a couple of times and so it was with a sad heart I felt I could not take the risk of going away with her any more.

Our friendship lasted for thirty years and I attended her seventieth, eightieth and ninetieth birthday parties – oh, and she did ask me to marry her a couple of times, the offer of which I tactfully declined. She told me she dreaded going into a care home, and the good Lord granted her that wish. In November 2010 I had a heart attack and spent a week in the Bristol Heart Institute. One afternoon I was sleeping and a nurse came and told me I had a visitor. I sat up and looked around and it was Alice in a wheelchair, being pushed by a porter, and in front was another porter pushing her shopping trolley. I was truly amazed that she made it and she told me she went to the porters' lodge and gave him my name and persuaded him to put her in the wheelchair and to get another porter to push her shopping trolley!

Of course after I left hospital, as soon as I was well enough I began to visit her again. I went there on Saturday night and found her unconscious in the corner of her bedroom. I checked to see if she was alive and called an ambulance, and also her friend Jenny Capstick from Broadmead Baptist Church, where she was at the time attending. Alice was duly taken to the BRI where she never really recovered consciousness.

I was officially her next of kin and I received a phone call from the BRI about five days after Christmas telling me that Alice was nearing her death, so I made haste to get there and sat with her for a number of hours, just touching her hand in the hope that she might realise I was there, but there was no response. I must have nodded off but woke with a start and somehow knew she had passed away.

Her funeral was amazing. The managers and staff of the shops she had visited attended as well as a wealth of friends and fellow church members. We had lunch in the Waddelow Hall at Broadmead Chapel and one of the things I did was to bring all her photo albums and invited everyone to browse through and take away any photos that they fancied.

The people of St Stephen's offered to allow Alice's ashes to be buried in the churchyard and the site was marked with a bay tree, which many years before I had purchased in Wilkinson's as a gift for her. All these years later when I meet her friends they still speak of her with love and respect and I know I was enriched by our long friendship and shall never forget her.

When I was about sixty-three years of age I developed hypertension with attacks of atrial fibrillation, probably due to the stress of running St Michael's Church. I also began to have uncontrollable nosebleeds, which usually resulted in hospitalisation for a few days. Eventually with the right medication the condition was brought under control, but I saw this as a warning that all was not well.

I am sure that my retirement and move to St Stephen's was a great help but I was also suffering from chronic breathlessness, the cause of which was a mystery to everyone, but I was really happy at the new church and at that time Christ Church was linked with St Stephen's. The priest in charge there was Maurice Turner and the church was a Book of Common Prayer church.

There was a lunchtime communion every Thursday and it had a very good choir of boys and men, with a good organist and a first-class organ. Then Edwin Morris, the rector of St Stephen's, retired and I did the short interregnum there until Peter Crick was appointed. I was also quite busy training and leading the team of guides at Bristol Cathedral.

For some reason my successor at St Michael's declined to take on the chaplaincy of Foster's and Colston's almshouses, so I still enjoyed those duties and in 1024 I began a second interregnum at St Stephen's, which lasted for two years.

Twenty-Seven

Shazdeh

Where Alice had lived in Carolina House there were four flats sharing a landing and quite often I met Shazdeh, because his flat faced on to the same landing as Alice's and one day he handed me a leaflet advertising himself as a gardener and handyman specialising in laminate flooring.

It was during the second year of my interregnum that John became ill and he actually died at the end of this period on January 19th. Our flat was looking very shabby and I have to admit that I am not the most enthusiastic of decorators, and even if I had suggested to John that something ought to be done, he always said he preferred it when I spent my time with him.

When John passed away my relatives were very good to me in the early days of bereavement and when things got too much for me they would put me up for a few days. I went on holiday and during that time they worked really hard at scrubbing and cleaning and repainting the walls, for which I paid them.

When I returned I had a new carpet fitted on the staircase and in the sitting room, and a new kitchen. The old 1950s wing chairs were thrown out and replaced with two leather bucket chairs; I bought a new fireplace, a new bed, two bedside cabinets and two basket chairs. This was all done because I was the sole beneficiary of John's will and I also sent money to each of John's relatives.

It was then that I decided that I would like to laminate the floor covering in the two bedrooms, so I contacted Shazdeh. He installed this for me and he did a thoroughly good job at a very reasonable price and we became good friends. I invited him to my eightieth birthday. Financially things were working out very well for me with the capital that was left and I was able to live on the interest.

Unfortunately it was not to last! The Wall Street crash had repercussions all round the world including the UK. Interest rates dropped so much that I began to use my capital. I talked about this to Shazdeh and said that I had decided to let one of my bedrooms to bring in some more income. He told me that sometime after he came to the UK, when he joined Stapleton Road Congregational Church, he discovered that once a week their hall was let out to refugees who got together socially, received advice, had haircuts and even a lunch, and that he became a helper there. He had met a young man named Hojat who was homeless and in the depths of despair and so he taken him into his home. Unlike Shazdeh, who worked and saved and even bought property and gained British citizenship, Hojat never really settled and longed for his home and relatives in Iran. Anyway, Shazdeh suggested that he and Hojat rented my bedroom and moved out of their flat and rented that out to someone else.

This seemed an ideal solution because among other things I had become progressively very breathless so that I had to get taxis to return home when I shopped in Broadmead, and it was costing me about £30 a week in taxi fares. The arrangement with Shazdeh and Hojat worked out very well because I was being looked after on a daily basis, although I know my brother and his wife were not keen on this idea at all.

I knew that because of my health I would need to look for a place to live that was without hills and very near shops and buses. One day Shazdeh and Hojat were doing a garden in Harcourt Hill and on the way home, at the bottom of Cranbrook Road and quite near

Gloucester Road, they spotted a ground floor flat for sale and told me about it.

I viewed the flat and fell in love with it. It was the ground floor and basement of a large Edwardian house built in 1903. There were two large rooms front and back, fourteen feet by fourteen feet and both with bay windows, and the front room still had the original ceiling coving and centrepiece. Then there were two smaller rooms, fourteen feet by eight feet, and one served as a kitchen. In the basement was another large room with French doors leading out on to a small garden. There was also a very large toilet and bathroom. The flat was beautifully decorated and had masses of power points. We figured out that Shazdeh would sleep in the large ground floor room and Hojat in the small room, and I chose to sleep in the basement room.

Shazdeh and I decided we would jointly purchase the property, so the money I put up was from the sale of the flat at Kingsdown and the remainder of my bank balance and Shazdeh put up some money and obtained a mortgage to make up the rest of the cost, which was about £275,000, and we moved in on February 19th 2010.

I decided to invite Alice to spend Christmas with us and for the first time she and I fell out because when I invited her she demanded to know who would also be with us and I told her that it would be just her, me, Shazdeh and Hojat. She was very rude and turned down my offer if they were present, so I made it clear it was my flat she was being invited to and it was my business who I invited, and I was really shocked at her attitude.

For some time I cut her dead and didn't see her, then Shazdeh met Alice in her flat in Fremantle Road and she wanted to know why I was not in contact with her. There is never any messing about with Shazdeh and he told her straight that her behaviour deeply offended me and she asked what she should do. Shazdeh suggested that she phone me and apologise for her rude behaviour. She did this and now of course I put everything behind us.

We soon learned that the first-floor flat was owned by a very awkward man who had originally moved in during the 1950s with his parents and they bought the whole house. At the same time they had to divide the house into two flats and they sold off the lower one, but I don't think this man ever reconciled himself to this and subconsciously he acted as if he were the landlord of our flat.

As well as running a self-employed gardening business and caring for Hojat and me, Shazdeh began a long programme of the renovating of our flat, which lasted until 2014. The first thing he did in the spring of 2010 was to excavate a large pond for me and stock it with koi fish, which gave me endless pleasure and they are still flourishing.

He was very good to Hojat, who worked in a fish and chip shop in Brislington, and Shazdeh took money from him, which he banked for him. Although Shazdeh had obtained British citizenship and had a British passport Hojat's heart was never really here; he spent most of his off-duty hours using the computer to daily contact his family, and when later in the year he learned that his father's illness was fatal he decided to return to Iran to be with his father before he died. Shazdeh had saved a large sum of money for him and he gave it to him so he could get established in Iran. So with heavy hearts we saw him off at Heathrow Airport.

In many ways 2010 was a very difficult year because for one thing I suffered a heart attack and developed pneumonia with it in October. I was operated on and cared for in the Bristol Heart Institute. I would like to put on record that the treatment and the aftercare there were superb and I made a good recovery. The second thing was that Alice was taken ill and passed away in the BRI at Christmastime.

In October we held a birthday party for Shazdeh in our front room and during the evening there was some dancing. I was sitting on the sofa opposite the fireplace and to my great alarm saw that our large aquarium in the recess to the right of the fireplace was, together with the floor on that side of the room, bouncing up and down! We decided the following day to take up the carpet on that side of the sitting room to look at the floor joists and when we did this, to our horror we discovered that each joist had rotted away where it joined the wall and there were masses of bricks piled to within a few inches of the floor.

Carpenters were called in to look at the floor and to work out how to repair it and their verdict was that before anything could be done, all the rubble beneath the floor would need to be removed to give them access. Shazdeh made a hole in our inner basement hall that allowed this rubble to be removed and in total it filled twelve skips.

In the meantime our difficult neighbour upstairs phoned the council and informed them that massive excavation work was being undertaken by us in our basement and was undermining the property. Naturally officials descended on us and demanded an explanation but when they saw what was happening and the reason for it they agreed that although an awful lot of rubble had been removed there was a perfectly good reason for it. So they more or less said to ignore him and finish the job. What the carpenters actually did was install joist cradles along the wall and remove the rotten wood and splice in the new joists. They then removed a large stanchion, which had been taking the weight of our sitting room floor above. With the new joists in place the floor on that half of the room was about one and a half inches higher and level and sound.

When all the rubble was removed we discovered that the liquid effluent from the upstairs downpipe had been penetrating the wall for many years and had caused a problem with damp resulting in the issues with our sitting room floor, so ironically the person who complained to the council was the cause of the problem and he had to get experts to put this leakage right.

The advantage we gained was another large basement as big as our sitting room. Another space was discovered next to the one under the sitting room but this one housed the two mains electricity supply cables to both flats which, because the area was now accessible, presented a real danger to anyone who went into this space. Western Power were contacted and they came and made these supply cables safe by rerouting them.

Shazdeh always said that he would take care of me in my old age; he claimed that he was shocked at the way elderly people in this country were pushed into care homes and the responsibility of their care passed on to the local authorities. He claimed that in Iran families consider it an honour and a privilege to care for their elderly kinsfolk.

From what had unexpectedly been discovered in our basement, plans were forming to convert these newly discovered areas into rooms and let them out to provide enough income to enable Shazdeh to give up his gardening job and look after me full-time. So we formed a plan for the complete reconfiguration of the basement to install two wet rooms, by covering an extremely large bathroom and toilet.

We applied for and obtained planning permission to install windows in the newly discovered rooms and they were plastered and renovated to a standard fit for tenants. Shazdeh also installed a toilet-cum-wet room on the ground floor to save me having to go down to the basement. It took him some hard work and planning to complete the work and his tenacity, skill and patience were exemplary.

The man upstairs was as difficult as it was possible to be at every stage of the work. All in all we recorded four visits from local council inspectors as a result of his complaints, and each time they visited us they assured us that what was being done was legal and to an acceptable standard. Eventually, despite his obstinacy even he realised he was beaten and he put his flat on the market.

The sad thing was that the one really good feature of the building was that when it was originally converted into flats, an annex was built to house an access staircase to the upstairs flat, and it was built on the rear corner of the property. It was a great advantage to us because the original staircase to the top floor ran from our hall and this was removed, making our flat self-contained. It was a great disadvantage to the upstairs occupants because their front door was downstairs at our garden level and on entry there were four flights of stairs to get to the top flat, which would put potential buyers off.

His flat was also very dated so although Cranbrook Road is in a very desirable area, there were no takers.

Early in 2014 Shazdeh had paid off the mortgage he had taken out to buy into our flat and he made a very reasonable offer for the upstairs flat. He obtained another mortgage and bought the upstairs flat so now we own the whole house and the neighbours moved out on July 31st.

The major work that Shazdeh had undertaken was to extend the walkway at the side of the property on the level right to the rear of the building and take out a window halfway up the annex and install a new door there. This was a vast improvement because now there were only two flights of stairs to the top flat. A floor was installed at this level, creating a nice basement room beneath, and the space under the walkway was renovated, tiled throughout and another toilet added.

Now we have enough tenants to provide sufficient income to free Shazdeh to look after me full-time but he is still busy. He assisted a carpenter to cover the walkway and provide a conservatory, which helps keep the house dry and warm. His latest project was to remove a large chimney breast in our kitchen and make good design sense of it. The bottom two flights of stairs in the annex were removed, adapted and are now installed as the access to the garden from the walkway.

I cannot speak too highly of Shazdeh's enthusiasm, willingness to work and his enabling me to remain in my own home. It was at his insistence that I undertook to write the story of my life.

Twenty-Eight

Visit to Iran

The first step that Shazdeh and I had to take to enable us to visit Iran was for me to obtain a visa and for Shazdeh to apply for an Iranian passport as his had been lost and the authorities refused to accept the validity of his British passport. First of all he sent a passport photo of me to his family in Tehran and they had to forward this, together with a request for me to visit them, to the correct authorities in Iran.

When we knew this was OK the next step was for us to visit the Iranian Embassy to obtain my visa and Shazdeh's passport. The problem was that due to diplomatic relations between the UK and Iran being suspended the embassy in London was closed, so we had to fly to Dublin and visit the Iranian Embassy there to obtain the necessary documents.

Once this was successfully completed we purchased our air tickets via the internet and flew with Pegasus Airways, which is based in Turkey. We left home at 5am to catch the 6am coach to Victoria and then after a short wait we caught another coach to Stansted Airport and took a five-hour flight to Istanbul. There was a five-hour wait there and eventually we boarded a plane for another five-hour flight to Tehran.

The first thing that struck me on arrival was the very large portraits of the two imams who are the top Islamic clerics there. There was some kind of mix-up so that Shazdeh's relatives, who should have been there to meet us, were nowhere to be seen. I was entirely in Shazdeh's hands and he negotiated with a taxi driver who agreed to drive us into Tehran and find a hotel for us.

We found one just as it was getting light, so we booked in, had a light breakfast and then crashed out in our room for a few hours. I must say that at that time I was anxious that maybe we would have to return to the airport and try and book a flight back to the UK. However, Shazdeh came up with a plan.

When he was living in Tehran many years ago he had been of great help to a friend called Rezah, who was so grateful that he told Shazdeh that if in the future he needed help he should call him, so that's what he did. Within a few hours Rezah and his wife came to the hotel and insisted that we be their guests for the fortnight that we were in Tehran and took us to their home.

There were three reasons that we went to Tehran – one, to visit Shazdeh's family; two, for Shazdeh to get a nose job as for many years, due to an injury to his nose he suffered from a blocked nostril. He had this corrected and they also reshaped his nose. And three, Shazdeh also needed a lot of treatment for his teeth. In fact the dentist fitted him with implants and both of these treatments were carried out efficiently and at a fraction of the cost they would have commanded in the UK. I have a top part of a denture which has never been satisfactory and for £50 the dentist there fitted me with an extra tooth and also did some adjustments which are entirely satisfactory.

The family we stayed with consisted of a husband and wife and a son and daughter, both of whom are studying and would like to attend university. It states quite clearly on my visa and on Shazdeh's passport that Iran is an Islamic republic and this is made very obvious by the many large portraits of the Islamic clerics which are seen everywhere in the city, even in banks, shops and offices.

Having stated this, I was amazed at the interest, kindness and obvious pleasure of everyone at meeting us and although Shazdeh made no secret of the fact that I was a retired priest, without exception everyone treated me kindly and with respect. Sadly, due to broken diplomatic relations it is an extremely rare event for anyone from the UK to visit Iran. At times I think Shazdeh paraded me like a treasured trophy. I was very impressed by the respect shown to elderly people and they seemed genuinely pleased to meet and talk to an eighty-four-year-old gentleman from the UK.

Rezah rode a very powerful motorbike and in Iran you are allowed to have two people riding pillion so we whizzed around Tehran on the back of his motorbike. I wore my straw hat à la bowling green! The traffic goes at a tremendous speed and is very dense but there seems to be no aggro between drivers.

In many parts of the city, instead of gutters there are little streams running and all the streets are lined with closely packed trees that grow in the streams, which is a good way of keeping them watered in the summer months.

The bread, which is purchased daily at local bakeries, is rather like pitta bread and is in large, crisp portions about eighteen by nine inches, and it is quite strange to see people collecting their bread in piles of about eighteen and held like trays in their hands. Breakfast was usually various cheeses, jam and honey and everyone broke off pieces of bread and wrapped it around whatever they were eating.

A lot of tea was consumed, fairly weak and in glasses, and most people popped one or two cubes of sugar in their mouths and sucked tea through them. There was usually a cooked meal in the evening with basmati rice as a base for what they called stew added. I was never quite sure what it was but I enjoyed it and the diet totally agreed with me.

A few people sleep on the floor on a kind of kapok mattress and they wrap themselves in duvets; it was a bit like camping indoors. However, I coped OK and slept well. The apartment we stayed in had a flat roof and I was told that they slept up there if the weather was very hot.

I think the biggest problem was that the toilet was simply a hole in the floor. People tend not to use toilet paper but use a bidet, both for washing after toileting and flushing. I get vertigo so it doesn't take much imagination to envisage my trepidation over this, but they kindly supplied me with my own toilet roll.

I think that due to staying with Shazdeh's friends and visiting his relatives we probably made more contact with Iranian people than if we had stayed in a hotel and done run-of-the-mill touristy things. Rezah was friendly with an estate agent who used to bring large boxes of fabulous cakes for us.

A couple of times we visited a bazaar, which was enormous and appeared to sell everything except fish and meat. You could purchase green or black mulberries and in one shop we visited you could buy dates, figs, dried apricots and sweets of dried plums, pecan nuts and many spices. The shopkeeper was very sociable and urged us to sample his goods, and I can still smell the intoxicating aromas of that shop. The bazaar also sold clothes, watches and jewellery. I bought two pairs of very nice shoes, which are as comfortable as moccasins, for about £2 per pair.

The women in Iran seem quite liberated; although you do see ladies wearing traditional clothes many of them wear Western dress, but they seem to favour exotic scarves and you do see them driving cars. We visited a small park and on the seats were groups of either men or women but they never appeared to mix.

When we visited anyone, the lady of the house would greet us at the door and once we removed our shoes and entered, the man of the house would introduce himself and engage in conversation while his wife would prepare and set before us a variety of fruit and sweets and the inevitable tea.

Some of the ladies wore a robe that was similar to the burka but was of a beautiful flowered material. It was worn in such a way that you could only see the ladies' faces and hands. I asked Shazdeh if this traditional dress was always worn and he told me that it was only worn in front of visitors or strangers.

Although Iran is a Muslim state I was surprised at their openness towards Christianity. For example, when we visited Shazdeh's family the youngest member, a little boy of just over a year old, was obviously unwell. The following day Shazdeh received a phone call saying that the little boy had been taken into hospital with a severe lung infection, and although they knew I was a retired Christian priest they asked for my prayers. I am glad to say that within a week the little boy was better and they were so grateful for my prayers. This request for my prayers recurred many times and when I left Rezah gave me a crucifix.

He also discovered from Shazdeh that I liked chips and so he cooked them especially for me every day. Although he could not speak English he would give me a knowing look and say, "Des cheeps" and peel the potatoes and fry them for me.

Although there are no large supermarkets in Tehran like Tesco or Sainsbury's there are a few fairly small ones. We visited one because we understood that the bakery department sold an Iranian take on doughnuts, although they were vastly different from what we know as doughnuts. Even there the baker was delighted to see me and invited me behind his counter to be photographed with him.

We visited Rezah's mother-in-law, a lady about seventy years old, and it was obvious she was not particularly well-off but she entertained us very well and found two pairs of nail clippers as presents for us. On the way back from her apartment we passed the Azadi Memorial at about 10pm. It is a huge octagonal triumphal arch erected during the Shah's reign. It was beautifully floodlit with an ever-changing display of colours.

We stopped the car but the traffic was horrendous and I could not see any way of crossing the road to get close to it. However, Shazdeh had a word with the police and told them about me, then they shook hands with me and formed a cordon and stopped all the traffic to allow us to get across the road and we saw the monument at close quarters.

Another highlight of the visit was to a time museum, which was housed in a historic mansion. There were clocks from all periods and from all around the world. Even without the exhibits the building was quite spectacular. The architecture of Tehran is very striking – unlike the UK, where the Georgian period gave us cities like Bath and the uniform terraces and squares which have influenced town development to this day, Tehran's architecture is a kind of Asiatic version of Art Deco, very striking in its own way.

We visited a bank one day and the security policeman was very interested in me, and as we left he came into the street to see us off. It was obvious he was totally gobsmacked to see an eighty-four-year-old gent get on the back of a motorbike and whizz off. Another day as we travelled round the city a motorbike carrying three young Iranians drew up alongside us and shouted greetings.

We visited a famous tourist site right up in the mountains, which consisted of many restaurants and cafes set each side of a winding, steep hill. On another occasion we went to a famous restaurant, which sits alongside a mountain stream. It was arranged as a series of cubicles, each large enough to accommodate a family party. Each cubicle consists of a large carpet surrounded by cushions so everyone sits on the floor to eat. We selected our food and then someone came to us with a kind of incense burner.

I ordered salmon with stuffed olives, which was delicious, and after the food was served, a hubble-bubble was brought to us and we all smoked. Then the proprietor, on being told my age and nationality, came and greeted me and I was photographed with all the staff. Many of the customers also came and spoke to me.

The day that we paid the visit was Pentecost Sunday, and both Shazdeh and I knew the great significance of it to the Christian church. I had also told him that my favourite hymn is 'Come, Holy Ghost, Our Souls Inspire', and that the tune is over a thousand years old and I know all the words. We were travelling home in the car with Rezah and his family and Shazdeh told them about Pentecost and the significance of this hymn to me, and that he was sure I would be willing to sing it to them. So I ended up with the extraordinary experience of singing an ancient Christian hymn to Shazdeh and three Muslims as we drove through Tehran.

As a gift to bring home, the family we stayed with gave us a large terracotta water feature to install in our pond and also a table lamp made from rock salt. To sum up, I think it was the most enjoyable and educational holiday I have ever experienced and I came back with a totally new opinion both of Iran and its wonderful people. I am also deeply grateful to Shazdeh, who made this visit possible and took such care of me.

It was the following year that the difficult neighbour upstairs sold his flat to us at a greatly reduced rate and moved out at the beginning of August. Most of the work to the side entrance was completed by the end of the year, so we booked another visit to Iran in the spring of 2015.

Twenty-Nine

Operation for Hip Replacement

On February 14th we were invited to lunch with some Polish friends, and when we arrived the driver parked the car and every-one got out. I should have waited until Shazdeh came to my door to help me out, but I didn't wait for him and opened the door on my own and fell out on to the path. Everyone rushed round to pick me up but somehow I knew that I had done some serious damage to myself.

Although I was not in pain, all the feeling had gone from my left leg, and my left foot was flopping about and I had no control over it. The people around me wanted to get me to my feet but I told them to make me comfortable where I was and to call an ambulance. They came and took me to Southmead Hospital A&E, where they X-rayed my leg and diagnosed a broken hip.

Since my heart attack I always carry my diary with me, which notes all my medications. When the doctors looked at it they discovered I was taking warfarin, so they were unable to operate immediately and put me in a ward and administered drugs to nullify the anticoagulant effect of the warfarin, and also gave me morphine to control the pain. While in hospital there were quite a lot of drugs administered to me, including the morphine, which on one occasion led me to hallucinate in the small hours of the night, which was quite alarming.

It took two days before they could operate and on February 16th I was given a partial hip replacement. My eighty-sixth birthday was on the 18th February and Shazdeh and a few friends visited me, and while they were there a small group of musicians stood outside my room playing their instruments. Shazdeh went out and told them that it was my birthday and they came into my room and everyone sang 'Happy Birthday' to me.

One of my visitors that day was Cedric Trotman, who had got to know John many years before when they both worked in Bristol Magistrates' Court, so I knew him second-hand through John. He brought me a book by Archbishop Desmond Tutu called *In God's Hands*, and reading the book made my stay in hospital not only tolerable but very worthwhile and led to my complete spiritual renewal.

A broken hip and its replacement is a very serious, painful condition and the recovery afterwards is quite a long process and involves a lot of physiotherapy and liberal use of painkillers and other medication. For example, after my operation I had to learn to walk again with the aid of a Zimmer frame. I struggled around like a toddler just learning to walk.

Even assuming that the hospital staff are brilliant (which in my case they were), the patient has to make a real effort in the process of rehabilitation, which I think I did because I was transferred to rehab quite soon after the operation. All in all I was hospitalised for fourteen days.

Before I was discharged workmen visited my home to install grab handles where there were steps and a steadying bar in my shower unit. The district nurses visited me daily to dress the wound and give me injections. I did improve rapidly and within two weeks was able to dispense with the Zimmer frame and use sticks, and began to be taken out by Shazdeh for very short walks as I gained strength.

Thirty

Cedric

Quite gradually I got to know Cedric and understand him better and I greatly respect him as one of my special friends. He was born and brought up in the Wye Valley village of St Briavels. His mother was a member of the local Anglican church and I suspect from what he told me that from a very early age he had a gender problem. Of course, sadly in those days it was a taboo subject and so the victim had to suffer in silence.

On one occasion there was an opportunity for Cedric to open up to his mother about his problem, but he failed to do this and from then on his life was one of repression. Part of his problem was that he was not overtly feminine and in the early days, I for one didn't detect any outward signs of a gender problem. Only someone who has this problem can fully understand it but I suspect it was not about sexuality, as with homosexuals or lesbians, but that the problem goes a lot deeper than that.

Men are generally about dominance, aggression and competition and that is why men fight and cause wars, whereas women are more about human values and an ability to multitask and form relationships. So I think Cedric must have wrestled with this problem most of his life and been very lonely and unhappy because of it.

But he has qualities that I greatly admire and Shazdeh feels the same empathy for him as well. For example, he annually copes at Christmastime with a lonely lady and devotes the whole couple of days to entertaining her and making her happy. When he buys greeting cards you can always tell that he has gone to endless trouble to get the right card for the right person and there is always a thoughtful and surprising message included, and the same goes for his presents.

I think we both have different theologies about the nature of God but we respect each other's views rather than bickering about them. Cedric also faithfully visits the graves of his family and friends at appropriate times during the year.

Quite recently (thank God) he has undergone therapeutic consultation with experts and is now in the process of preparing for a medically led gender reassignment procedure. I am delighted that he is gradually becoming a happier and more contented person because he deserves the peace and contentment that most of us take for granted. At present he/she is wearing ladies' clothes and is now known as Julienne, but I know that Shazdeh and I and Jenny Capstick share a great affection for him/her and admire her for what she is undertaking.

Thirty-One

Second Visit to Iran and Final Thoughts

When we booked our second holiday in Iran at the beginning of the year, we did not of course anticipate my accident on February 14th and I really thought we would have to cancel it because our outward flight was on May 14th. However, I made such progress that we decided to go ahead, but with hindsight I don't think it was such a good idea because I was ill most of the time we were there and I didn't recover until we arrived home.

Nonetheless, between the bouts of sickness we travelled on the Tehran underground system, which is very modern (unlike the Tube in London) and everyone is chatty and friendly. I sat next to a young lady who had a small child on her lap who was obviously interested in me, and she placed the child on my lap and people in the compartment crowded around and took our photos and shook hands with me.

We travelled on an overnight sleeper and everyone in the compartment shared their food and asked about Shazdeh and me. One day we visited a farm, which was totally unlike an English farm because in that particular area there was no rainfall and so it was by nature a desert, but where crops were cultivated there were deep wells with pumps that brought the water to the surface and into irrigation channels which surround all the areas growing crops.

Back in Tehran, one afternoon I was taken to an open-air festival in a park where there were about a thousand people present enjoying themselves. At the end of the proceedings an MC got on to the stage to wrap everything up and asked if there were any visitors from abroad present. My hosts put up their hands and pointed to me, so I was asked to stand up and everyone applauded me.

Later in the summer I returned to Southmead Hospital for a hernia repair, which was carried out under local anaesthetic. I was on the operating table for about one hour and didn't feel a thing although I was fully conscious, but there was a screen so that I could not actually see what they were doing. It was all very informal and now and again the surgeon checked to make sure I was OK. I was kept in hospital overnight just in case I had a post-operative bleed but was discharged the following morning.

Looking back on my life I consider I have been very fortunate both in the opportunities presented to me, and the many good people I have met on my long journey. I cannot claim to have been a particularly good Christian but above all what I cherish most is my relationship with God, and more than that, His love and goodness to me.

Quite recently I have become a member of Stapleton Road Congregational Chapel, and my reason for this is because I attend this church quite a lot. I started doing so purely to support Shazdeh because it is his church, but really I attended as a visitor to begin with.

I have discovered such a depth of Christian love between the people there, and this same love has been generously shown to me. Also, I greatly admire the hard work and Christian example of the leaders, especially Keith and Pam Dix.

As a result of this I felt led to ask to become more than a visitor and so I am now a member of that church.

Acknowledgements

My thanks go to Farid Nikbakht Nejad (Shazdeh), who patientry listened to my life stories and stated that I should write a book about it. Also to Pam Dix who read my manuscript and typed it in a form acceptable to my publishers.

Lightning Source UK Ltd.
Milton Keynes UK
UKOW01f0627240317
297400UK00002B/25/P